Focke Wulf 190
AT WAR

Focke Wulf 190
AT WAR

Alfred Price FRHistS

Charles Scribner's Sons
NEW YORK

Printed in Great Britain
Library of Congress Catalog Card Number 77-78704
ISBN 0-684-15323-8

Contents

Foreword
Generalleutnant a. D. Adolf Galland

When Alfred Price asked me to write this foreword, my first thought was: 'I suppose it will be yet another technical account of this aircraft, somebody once again listing the minute differences between the various sub-types.' How pleased I was to be proved wrong. The author is a flying man himself, and he has collected in *Focke Wulf 190 at War* some fascinating stories about flying men, intended primarily for flying and ex-flying readers.

When I flew the FW190 for the first time, in 1942, I remember being greatly impressed by its high performance and its beautiful handling characteristics. So I was extremely interested to have my memories re-awakened after all these years when reading the comprehensive report written on this aircraft by the former enemy. We in the Luftwaffe knew that the FW190 was good, but in 1941 and 1942 we had no way of knowing that it was causing the enemy quite so much worry. Also of great interest to me was the British plan to mount an operation to hijack an FW190 from one of our airfields in France; the airfield at Abbeville was the home of II.Gruppe of Jagdgeschwader 26, my former unit. Had the hijack operation been carried out the plan would have placed considerable risks on the men involved; but it has to be admitted that the chances of success were high enough to justify such risks in wartime.

I may mention a not very serious criticism of this excellent and most interesting book: I should have preferred that a fighter *Gesch-wader* or *Division* commander, with a more extensive overall knowledge, should have been given the chance to contribute a section.

In this book the reader is able to sense the crushing pressure exerted on the Luftwaffe during the final year of the war, as the heavily outnumbered German fighter and fighter-bomber units, gradually dwindling in operational strength as losses in trained men were no longer made good and the last remaining petrol stocks were consumed, were hounded down both in the air and on the ground. It provides a grim reminder of the penalties suffered when an enemy gains air supremacy over one's homeland, penalties which no German who experienced them will ever forget. Let us be sure that, whatever else we chose to learn from the lessons of the past, the vital necessity of strength in the air should never be far from our minds.

I wish Alfred Price success for his new book, because his painstaking research and careful collation deserve it.

Introduction

Of the fighters which saw service in the Luftwaffe during the Second World War, none caused its enemies a nastier shock than did the Focke Wulf 190. When it first became operational, in the autumn of 1941, this aircraft could out-run, out-climb and out-dive the Spitfire V, the best fighter the Royal Air Force then had. Only with its tighter turning circle did the Spitfire have a slight edge and even this advantage was tempered by the fact that the German fighter had a superior rate of roll.

So much better than the Spitfire did the FW190 appear, that Royal Air Force pilots began to ascribe to it an excellence even greater than it merited. Indeed had the Commander-in-Chief of RAF Fighter Command, Air Chief Marshal Sir Sholto Douglas, been asked in the spring of 1942 what he wanted most of all for his force, it is probable that he would have answered: 'A few squadrons of Focke Wulf 190s!'

Plans were even laid to mount a commando operation to seize an example of the new fighter (see 'To Hijack a Focke Wulf'), so that British designers might discover its secrets. The plans were almost immediately overtaken by events, however, for in June 1942 a lost German pilot presented the Royal Air Force with an intact example of the FW190. The subsequent flight trials carried out in Britain (see 'Unsolicited Testimonials') revealed the FW190 for what it was: a brilliantly designed high performance fighter, with a few weaknesses but not many.

That the FW190 was so greatly superior in performance to the Spitfire V was remarkable enough. Yet more remarkable was the fact that (as he says in 'Concept to Fruition'), Kurt Tank had designed his fighter not as a 'racehorse' for which all was sacrificed in the name of performance. His intention had been to build what he termed a 'cavalry horse': a rugged fighting machine that would be able to take punishment as well as dish it out.

It is a truism in war, however, that one learns far more from a defeat than from a victory. Shocked to the core by the revelation that their fighters had been proved inferior to those of the enemy, aircraft firms in Britain, the USA and Russia were pressed to build aircraft able to match and even surpass the FW190 in fighting prowess.

The period during which the FW190 enjoyed a clear superiority over all comers lasted for about a year. Then in the summer of 1942 the hastily-introduced Mark IX version of the Spitfire, fitted with a new engine with two-stage supercharging, began to enter service; if well handled it could give the FW190 a hard fight, particularly at high altitude. From then until the end of the war the best of the Allied fighters were broadly comparable with the latest versions of the FW190, and the Tank 152 which followed it.

A rugged high performance aircraft, the FW190 made a very good fighter-bomber (see 'Mediterranean Jabo' and 'Eastern Front Jabo'). It was also pressed into service as an improvised night fighter and as a reconnaissance fighter.

During the second half of the war the German forces were thrown on to the defensive on each front in turn, as the overwhelming Allied superiority in manpower and resources began to take effect. So far as the fighter and fighter-bomber units equipped with the FW190 were concerned, this affected them in two ways. Firstly, they found themselves confronted by enemies vastly superior in numbers and flying aircraft comparable in quality. Secondly, as the war of attrition ran its bloody course and the well-trained German pilots of the early war period were killed, wounded or taken prisoner, their places in the front-line units were taken by pilots less well prepared for the rigours of combat. As the war progressed the quality of the training of the German fighter pilots declined steadily, while that of their Allied counterparts improved. Superior numbers and better training gave the Allied fighter pilots a mighty advantage, which untutored resolution and personal self-sacrifice could rarely redress (see 'No Place for a Beginner').

From the beginning of 1944 the Luftwaffe found itself engaged in a life-and-death struggle to defend the German homeland against the powerful American bomber attacks. The heavily armed and armoured bombers proved difficult to knock down, however. After many expedients had been

Left: The author (right) pictured with the designer of the Focke Wulf 190, Kurt Tank (centre) at Celle while collecting material for this book. On the left is Bernhard Jope, one of those who flew the unusual *Beethoven* combination.

tried, the answer appeared in the form of stoutly-armoured FW190s equipped with heavy cannon; these aircraft were issued to the so-called *Sturmgruppen*, whose pilots were pledged initially to press home their attacks to close range and ram the bombers if they could not knock them down by conventional means (see 'If Necessary by Ramming').

The pressure on the Luftwaffe became crushing on all fronts during the final months of the war, as its units were squeezed back inexorably into the shrinking area under German control (see 'Night Jabo' and 'Finale'). Also during the closing stages of the conflict, the FW190 was used as the upper half of the remarkable *Beethoven* explosive aircraft (see 'An Introduction to Beethoven').

Between June 1941 and the end of the war a total of just under 20,000 Focke Wulf 190s were built; thus, in terms of the number produced, the fighter was surpassed only by the Messerschmitt 109 (more than 33,000 built), the Russian Yak series of fighters (about 30,000) and the British Spitfire (just over 22,000).

Acknowledgements

In writing this book I have been fortunate in receiving the generous assistance of many of those who knew the Focke Wulf 190 at first hand. First and foremost I should like to thank its designer, Dipl-Ing Professor Kurt Tank; he is still a busy man in the German aircraft industry but he generously spared me the time for an interview. I should also like to thank Dipl-Ing Hans Sander for his expert assistance; he flew the FW190 during its maiden flight and knows more than anyone else about the testing of this aircraft. Then there were the men who flew the FW190 in action: Adolf Dilg, Helmut Wenk, Werner Gail, Walther Hagenah, Fritz Buchholz, Ernst Schroeder, Oskar Romm and Franz Zueger. Finally I should like to thank my good friend Bernhard Jope for his account of flying the *Beethoven*.

Many good friends provided photographs and information for this work. In particular I am grateful to Hans-Justus Maier, the historian of the present Fokker-VFW Company; he could not have done more to assist. Other contributors were Hans Redemann, Hanfried Schliephake, Derek Wood, Werner Girbig, Guenther Heise, Franz Selinger, Jean-Bernard Frappe, Eddie Creek and J. Richard Smith. I am also grateful to the Bundesarchiv Bildarchiv at Koblenz for the use of their photographs, and to the Comptroller of the Public Record Office in London for permission to reproduce the British official documents used in this book. Cliff Minney did the line drawings.

Finally I hope that you, the reader, will have as much enjoyment in reading this book as I had in doing the research for it and putting it together.

Alfred Price

Concept to Fruition
Professor Dr Ing Kurt Tank

Of the men associated with the Focke Wulf 190 the name that springs most readily to peoples' minds is Kurt Tank, the firm's Technical Director at the time it was conceived. This is his story.

It was during the spring of 1938 that the Air Ministry in Berlin asked the Focke Wulf company to submit design proposals for a new fighter, to supplement the Messerschmitt 109 which had just entered service. My Project Office submitted several alternatives, all based round the idea of a fighter somewhat more rugged than the Messerschmitt 109. One of these proposals was accepted and we received an order to proceed with the construction of prototypes of the Focke Wulf 190.

The Messerschmitt 109 and the British Spitfire, the two fastest fighters in the world at the time we began work on the FW190, could both be summed up as a very large engine on the front of the smallest possible airframe; in each case armament had been added almost as an afterthought. These designs, both of which admittedly proved successful, could be likened to racehorses: given the right amount of pampering and an easy course, they could outrun almost anything. But the moment the going became tough they were liable to falter. During World War 1 I had served in the cavalry and in the infantry and I had seen the harsh conditions under which military equipment has to work in wartime. I felt sure that a quite different breed of fighter would also have a place in any future conflict: one that could operate from ill-prepared front line airfields; one that could be flown and maintained by men who had received only a short training; and one that could absorb a reasonable amount of battle damage and still get back. This was the background thinking behind the Focke Wulf 190;

Below: The prototype Focke Wulf 190, pictured in the experimental shop at Bremen during advanced assembly in the spring of 1939./*Weber*

it was to be not a 'racehorse' but a *Dienstpferd*, a cavalry horse.

Obviously, if it was fitted with an engine developing the same power, a 'racehorse' fighter with a lighter structure would always be able to out-run and out-climb the sort of fighter we had in mind; yet we could not allow this difference to become too great. The design problem centred round building a stronger airframe and one able to carry heavier weapons, without sacrificing too much in the way of flying performance.

The basic layout of the Focke Wulf 190 was entirely conventional: the monoplane with the nose-mounted engine driving a tractor airscrew was accepted at that time as being the most efficient layout for a high performance fighter. The low wing provided a convenient housing for the retractable undercarriage and meant that the legs could be kept short, and also gave a minimum of interference with the pilot's vision. From my own flying experience I knew how important it was for a fighter pilot to have the best possible all-round view and we decided to fit a large frameless bubble canopy to the new fighter; later these became very fashionable, but in 1938 the idea was something of an innovation.

We chose an air-cooled radial engine for the new fighter for two reasons: firstly, because such engines were far more rugged and could survive more punishment than the liquid-cooled types; and secondly, because the BMW company was bench-running prototypes of a new engine, the 1,550hp BMW 139, which developed somewhat more power than any liquid-cooled engine we had been offered. If our *Dienstpferd* was to come close in performance to other peoples' 'racehorses', we would need all the engine power we could get. Some people have suggested that I had to fight some sort of battle with the German Air Ministry to get them to accept the idea of a radial-engined fighter. That might make a good story but it is not history. In fact, there was quite a large body of official opinion in favour of such a fighter for the Luftwaffe. The Russian Rata fighter, several examples of which had been captured in Spain and brought back to Germany, had demonstrated the usefulness of a rugged fighter powered by an air-cooled engine. Looking further afield we saw that other nations, in particular the United States, were pushing ahead with the design and development of high-powered radial engines for fighters and we in Germany had no wish to lag behind in this field.

So the air-cooled radial engine was fitted to the FW190; I never had cause to regret the decision. When the fighter went into action the resilience of this type of power plant was proved again and again. There were several occasions when these fighters returned home and made normal landings, having actually had whole cylinders shot away; once its cooling system has been pierced and the liquid allowed to drain away, the running life of an equivalent liquid-cooled engine would have been about three minutes.

The design of the Focke Wulf 190 was, as in the case of all successful aircraft, very much a team effort. I dare say a really good designer could have produced such a fighter all by himself; but it would have taken about eight years and at the end of that time nobody would have been in the least bit interested in it! A design for a fighting aircraft was of value only if it could be brought out quickly. So the closest collaboration between the members of the design team was essential. My assistant, Willi Kaether, co-ordinated the work. Rudi Blaser with the help of the people in the drawing office designed the structure; he was a very clever practical engineer and usually seemed able to meet the strength requirement for a particular component for the lowest possible structural weight. Ludwig Mittelhueber headed the team at the Project Office responsible for the FW190. Hans Sander and Kurt Melhorn, the men who were to carry out the initial flying test programme, were brought in early and had a great deal of say, especially about the layout of the cockpit, the positioning of the instruments and the design of the controls. Altogether, the team which

Below: Kurt Tank in the cockpit of a FW190. He often took part in the flight test programmes of his own designs. *VFW-Fokker*

11

Right: Two views showing the first prototype nearing completion. The ducted spinner was fitted only to this example of the FW190./*via Redemann*

prepared the design of the FW190 comprised about twelve men.

By 1938 it was clear that the trend of future development would make military aircraft heavier and heavier; from the start, the FW190 had been designed to accept this trend. The effect of this line of thinking is best exemplified by the undercarriage. For the design weight and estimated landing speed of the prototype aircraft, we calculated that an undercarriage able to withstand a sinking speed of 8.5ft per sec would be sufficient. But if the aircraft was to be developed its maximum speed, weight and landing speed would all increase, resulting in considerably higher forces on the under-carriage during landing. So in the original stress calculations we allowed for a sinking speed not of 8.5 but of 15ft per sec; and then we designed the undercarriage to be strong enough to take that. The move paid off. During its life the maximum loaded weight of the FW190 rose from 2.75 tons to more than twice that figure, but with few changes the undercarriage remained adequate. I have used the undercarriage as an example, but in fact several parts of the original structure were a great deal stronger than the minimum necessary.

Although the new fighter had to be rugged, it had also to handle well in the air. The secret of this was to make the control surfaces large enough and to balance them with great care, both statistically and dynamically; if they were underbalanced they became too heavy and lost their effectiveness, if they were overbalanced one was liable to get other problems. We did a lot of work on the FW190 to get a positive and immediate response from the controls. Between the control column and the control surfaces we used rigid rods instead of the more usual wires and pulleys; the latter were liable to stretch and the resul-tant play caused a delay in the action of the controls.

Once the prototype of the new fighter was flying, late in the spring of 1939, we were able to explore the handling characteristics. Hans Sander did the initial testing, then I flew the aircraft and found that she handled beautifully in the air. The work we had put into the flying controls had produced the results we wanted. I have always believed that a pilot should not have to use a great deal of muscle power to get an aeroplane to do what he wants; if the controls have been properly designed he should be able to conduct most manoeuvres with only a finger and thumb on the stick. In combat a high rate of roll is essential for a fighter, so that the pilot can make rapid changes in his direction of flight. The aileron stick forces had, however, to be kept below a maximum of about eight pounds

because a man's wrist cannot exert a force much greater than that. We succeeded in getting the stick forces down and finally I had the aileron controls as I wanted them: the aircraft followed the movement of the stick immediately and precisely, with no initial tendency to yaw. Compared with the ailerons, the other flying controls were relatively easy to design: the stick forces were not so critical for the elevators and the highest forces of all could be taken on the rudder pedals, because a man's legs are far stronger than his arms.

Once we had the controls correctly balanced we had to see that they stayed that way over a wide range of speeds: a fighter pilot does not want to have to re-trim his aircraft every time he moves the throttle. In fact, we did not have movable trim tabs on the FW190. We used small fixed tabs on the ailerons, elevators and rudder that were adjusted on the ground to compensate for the wide tolerances one has to accept when an aircraft is mass-produced. The only trim available in flight was in the elevator sense, and that was provided by the all-moving tailplane.

The prototype FW190 flew well enough although there was some trouble with the BMW139 engine, whose rear cylinders were prone to over-heating. To reduce the drag of the radial engine to a minimum, the prototype was fitted with a special ducted spinner through which the cooling air passed; once the air had done its work it was ejected from the rear of the spinner under pressure, so that it provided a little extra thrust. Flight tests, however, suggested that the use of the ducted spinner gave little reduction in drag and the installation was not worth the bother. Early in the test programme we reverted to the more normal type of cowling for the radial engine.

Even before the prototype FW190 had begun its flight trials, the BMW company was offering the new BMW801 engine which was then undergoing bench testing. Quite apart from the promise of an extra 50hp initially, rising to 200hp extra later, the new engine looked like being more reliable and less liable to overheating than the BMW139 we had been using. Shortly after the first flight of the FW190, we received a contract to modify the design to enable it to take the BMW801. The resultant aircraft, the FW190V5, flew for the first time early in the spring of 1940. Although the extra 50hp was useful, we found that the extra 350lbs of engine weight, plus the weight of the addi-tional structure necessary to carry it, plus weight of the armour and the additional equipment which the Luftwaffe now wanted fitted, had increased the all-up weight by about a quarter. The wing loading rose from the 38lbs sqft of the first prototype to 46lbs sqft and turning performance deteriorated

accordingly. To restore the aircraft's previously pleasant handling characteristics we enlarged the wing by extending each tip by just over 20in and reducing the amount of taper so that the outer sections were somewhat wider. In this way we increased the wing area by just over 35sqft and lowered the wing loading to a more reasonable 35.8lbs sqft. Later, to maintain the correct relationship between the wing and the tailplane, we made a proportional increase in the area of the latter. The wing and the tailplane of the low and medium altitude versions of the FW190 then remained unchanged throughout the remainder of the development life of the aircraft.

At first we had some cooling problems with the BMW801, though they were not so serious as those of the BMW139 and they were soon reduced to within acceptable limits. Far more serious were the troubles we experienced with the so-called *Kommandogeraet* for the BMW801. This was a rather clever device intended to save the pilot having to worry about the optimum relationship between altitude and fuel flow, fuel mixture, propeller pitch setting, ignition timing, engine revolutions and the selection of the correct supercharger gear. The pilot had simply to move one control, his throttle, and in theory the *Kommandogeraet* did the rest. I say in theory, because at first the device did not work at all well. All sorts of things went wrong with it, one of the more disconcerting being the rather violent automatic switching-in of the high gear of the supercharger as the aircraft climbed through 8,700ft. On one occasion I was

carrying out a test with an early version of the FW190 which involved a loop at medium altitude. Just as I was nearing the top of the loop, on my back with little airspeed, I passed through 8,700ft and the high gear of the supercharger cut in with a jerk. The change in torque hurled the aircraft into a spin with such suddenness that I became completely disorientated; and since there was a ground haze and an overcast, and my artificial horizon had toppled, I had no way of knowing which way was 'up'. Indeed, I never did find out whether it was an upright or an inverted spin. After a lot of trial and error, and a considerable loss in altitude, I managed to recover from the spin. But the incident had given me a lot to think about. As soon as I landed I was on the telephone to the BMW company and I told them that if they did not sort out their engine and its terrible *Kommandogeraet*, I would do all in my power to see that somebody else's engine was fitted into the FW190! The *Kommandogeraet* was made to work and it worked very well, but it took quite a battle on our part.

When it went into action, in the summer of 1941, the FW190 soon demonstrated a clear margin of superiority over the enemy fighters confronting it. With its powerful radial engine, our *Dienstpferd* was treated with considerable respect by the enemy 'racehorses'. This situation lasted for about a year, until the Mark IX Spitfire became operational powered by a new version of the Merlin engine fitted with a two-stage supercharger; this aircraft had the edge over the FW190 at altitudes above 25,000ft. We tried

all sorts of things to improve the high altitude performance of the BMW801 and experimented with water-methanol injection and turbo-superchargers; but really a completely new engine was needed. I had foreseen that something like this might happen and early in 1941, even before the FW190 had entered service, I had spoken to Luftwaffe Generals Udet and Jeschonnek about the need to put the Jumo 213 high altitude engine, then being bench tested at Junkers, into series production so that we could have a high altitude version of the FW190 ready in case it was needed. General Hans Jeschonnek, then Chief of Staff of the Luftwaffe, had replied: 'What is the point of that? We are not fighting any air battles at high altitude!' The result was that we lost about a year in the development of an effective high altitude engine, which we never really made up. In the end we did get the FW190D into service powered by the liquid-cooled Jumo 213, and it made a very good high altitude fighter. But it was not ready until late in the summer of 1944, by which time the battle for air superiority over Germany had been lost.

The final development of the FW190 series of fighters to go into service, the Ta152, was powered by the Jumo 213E which with two-stage supercharging developed 1,730hp at altitudes above 35,000ft; this gave the fighter, which had a wing span lengthened to 47ft 6in for high altitude operations, a maximum speed of 472mph at 41,000ft – which is very close to the limits of what is possible, using a piston engine. On one occasion during the closing stages of the war I was flying a Ta152

and had just taken off from Lagenhagen near Hanover on my way to a conference at Kottbus. Suddenly the control tower called me and informed me that there were '*Zwei Indiana ueber dem Gartenzaun*' – two enemy fighters over the airfield. This placed me in a difficult position because, anxious to remain a 'civilian', I never flew with loaded guns. One could hardly expect the pilots of the two Mustangs to know that, however, and it is doubtful whether they would have acted any differently if they had known. As they came boring down after me I rammed open the throttle and switched in the water methanol injection. My aircraft surged forwards, accelerating rapidly. The Mustangs' closing speed swiftly fell to zero, then they diminished in size until they were mere specks in the distance. I have often wondered what those American pilots thought had happened to their 'sitting duck'. The Ta152 became operational just before the war ended, but it never really had the chance to prove itself in action.

There is little doubt that the *Dienstpferd* concept, upon which the Focke Wulf 190 was based, was sound. Soon after the war I was invited to the Society of British Aircraft Constructors' Display at Hatfield. I was walking into the Rolls-Royce chalet and amongst the people there was the RAF fighter ace Johnny Johnson. When we were introduced, he commented 'Oh, so you are the man responsible for the fighter which gave us all such a twitch in 1942 . . . '

Initial Flight Testing
Dipl-Ing Hans Sander

Once an aircraft has been built, it falls to the test pilots to discover any hidden vices or faults and to establish its performance envelope. In this section Hans Sander gives a fascinating insight into the testing of the prototype of the Focke Wulf 190.

I first became interested in aeronautics in 1928, while studying mechanical engineering at the Technical High School at Aachen. I joined the academic flying group there and learned to fly; later I designed a high-performance glider, the FVA9, and took part in its construction. In 1934, after gaining my degree as a Diploma Engineer, I entered the German Research Institute for Aeronautics (DVL) in Berlin for training as a *Flugbaumeister*. (Broadly the equivalent of the modern Project Engineer – author.)

The three-year *Flugbaumeister* course was extremely thorough and included 15 months working at the flight test centre at Rechlin as an engineering test pilot. While there, I had the chance to try my hand flying almost every modern aircraft type at the centre. I completed my course successfully and in April 1937 I was offered the post of development test pilot at the Focke Wulf factory. During the years that followed I took part in the testing of the company's latest aircraft: the FW187 heavy fighter, the FW189 reconnaissance machine and the four-engined FW200 transport.

By the time the Focke Wulf 190 was taking shape, I was head of the firm's prototype flight test department. From the very beginning, I was involved with the new fighter. I was there when we designed and built the wooden mock-up to see that everything would fit in and I had a lot to do with the cockpit layout. Then the first pieces of metal were cut and as she gradually took shape I came to know her intimately. By the middle of May 1939 the new fighter was complete and we carried out the engine-running trials. Then I

Below: The first prototype FW190, pictured at about the time of its maiden flight. During its initial trials this aircraft carried the civil registration D-OPZE./*via Redemann*

conducted the taxi-ing trials – which proved very little, because the small works airfield at Bremen did not allow much of a ground run if one was to stop before hitting the fence at the other end. By this stage, however, I knew the aircraft so well that I was completely confident that she would fly safely when the time came.

On 1st June everything was ready and the prototype was wheeled out for her maiden flight. I started the engine and taxied out to the end of the runway. Then, after a final detailed check that everything was as it should be, I pushed open the throttle. With 1,550hp pulling it the aircraft surged forwards, accelerating rapidly to flying speed. At a speed of just over 100mph, she lifted off the ground and climbed away.

At that time a retractable undercarriage was still something of a novelty. People still did not trust them to work properly and it was usual for an aircraft making its first flight to do so with the undercarriage locked down. During the first flight of the FW190, however, I had to weigh the chances of undercarriage failure against those of an engine failure at low altitude. If I was unable to glide back to the airfield I should have to make an emergency landing in one of the neighbouring fields; and if the surface was not flat a wheels-down landing might result in the aircraft nosing over and ending up on its back. Immediately after take-off, I retracted the undercarriage of the FW190.

Once airborne I spiralled up to about 6,000 feet, keeping close overhead the airfield so that those on the ground could see what was happening. I made a couple of high speed runs to see how she handled close to her maximum speed, then turns at different speeds and noted the stick forces that were necessary. Aerodynamically, she handled beautifully. The controls were light, positive and well-balanced and throughout the initial flight I never once had to make use of the tailplane trim. I suppose most test pilots would have made at least a roll in the new aircraft, but I did no aerobatics during the maiden flight of the FW190; I was quite happy to leave such fancy flying until later in the test programme, when I knew a little more about her. At this stage my task was merely to 'taste' the handling characteristics of the new fighter.

For the first flight I wore only a thin flying suit over my normal underwear, socks, ordinary shoes, and a flying helmet with my oxygen mask hanging loose. Yet soon after take-off I began to sweat profusely. The rear of the engine was hard up against the front wall of the cockpit, and my feet on the rudder pedals were either side of the engine accessories. The temperature in the cockpit rose to 55°C; I felt as though I was sitting with my feet in a fire! The heat was bearable, but very uncomfortable. Potentially more dangerous was the fact that the sealing round the cockpit was poor in places, and the exhaust fumes began to seep in. Fortunately I always flew with my oxygen mask close to hand (ever since a near-disaster at Rechlin, when I suffered a severe dose of carbon monoxide poisoning whose effects lasted for about six months). I clamped my mask to my face and made almost the whole of the maiden flight breathing pure oxygen.

A further problem was caused by the undercarriage retraction mechanism: the up-lock did not engage properly. If I pulled any 'G' the undercarriage legs were liable to sag down and in the cockpit the red 'undercarriage unlocked' light came on. The prototype FW190 was fitted with a hydraulic retraction system (on later production aircraft it was electrical) and during its operation the hydraulic system ran at an overload pressure of about 1700lbs sqin; I knew that if I operated it at this overload pressure too often, to get the undercarriage to lock up again, the hydraulic pump was liable to break down. The system had to be treated with care. This was a minor problem, however, nothing more.

After about twenty minutes at medium altitude, the time came to try the first landing. To leave as little as possible to chance, before descending I made a couple of stalls and a simulated landing, to see whether her low speed handling characteristics were normal.

Below: Hans Sander at the controls of an FW190. He flew this aircraft during its maiden flight and played a major part in its testing during the years that followed./*Sander*

They were. Then I throttled back and went down, extended the flaps and undercarriage and made a perfectly ordinary landing. There was no drama of any sort – drama is the last thing a test pilot wants with a new aircraft.

As soon as the prototype was back in the hangar after the flight, I had her put up on jacks to try and sort out the trouble with the up-lock. I saw the cause of the trouble: the locking catch was not engaging the lug on the undercarriage leg properly. So I filed away some of the metal from the inside of the catch, a move which reduced but did not eliminate the incidence of unlocking during subsequent test flights. We also tightened up the up-lock mechanism more and more, until one day I was faced with the opposite problem: prior to landing at Rechlin in the prototype on 3 July, where I was to give a demonstration before Goering and Udet, I released the up-lock before extending the undercarriage – and found it would not budge! Fortunately I knew the system well enough to be able to 'trick' it and get my wheels down. Once on the ground at Rechlin I had the aircraft jacked up and re-adjusted the up-lock mechanism; the demonstration afterwards went off perfectly. But the incident could have given rise to a difficult situation at the worst possible time.

The basic reason for the poor performance of the up-lock mechanism was that it simply was not strong enough for the job it had to do: the catch itself was cut out of a piece of sheet metal and was operated by a simple wire cable. I became convinced that such a mechanism would never be suitable for mass production. After a lot of discussion we removed the locking catch altogether and substituted a bomb release shackle; that proved more than strong enough for the job and we had no further trouble.

Another difficulty that manifested itself during the test programme concerned the cockpit canopy opening system: it was quite impossible to get the hood open when flying at speeds above about 270mph. This meant that I could not abandon the aircraft if there was an emergency at high speed – not the sort of prospect to cheer any pilot flying an unproven aircraft. No matter how hard one tried to wind open the hood using the winding mechanism provided, the aerodynamic forces pushing forwards held it firmly closed. Rudi Blaser worked out a new system using bungee rubber to assist in opening the hood but that did not work either: when operated at high speed the hood would open a little, then slam shut. Next he tried a more powerful system using compressed air, but that was little better. Gradually it became clear that we needed to know more about the aerodynamic forces round the canopy so we fitted sensors

Far left, top: With Hans Sander at the controls, the first prototype FW190 is seen during flight trials after the removal of the original ducted spinner and its replacement with a more conventional radial cowling. *VFW-Fokker*

Hans Sander's ejector seat: *Far left, bottom:* lowering the correctly weighted dummy pilot into the cockpit; *Above:* in position; *Centre left:* during firing; *Below left:* caught by the wooden structure protecting the tail. The aircraft used in this trial was the twenty-second A-O pre-production aircraft. *VFW-Fokker*

to take pressure measurements at high speed. From these we calculated that about 50hp would be necessary to overcome the forces holding the canopy shut; power of a somewhat higher order than previously used would be necessary if it was to be wrenched open. Finally Blaser designed a new system using a 20mm cartridge firing against a piston, to push the canopy rearwards and force it to jettison cleanly. The first time we tried out the system on the ground we did not lose the canopy, we lost the piston! The force of the explosion tore the piston away from the hood and it emerged from the fuselage at high speed. Fortunately, nobody was in the way! Fitted with stronger attachment points, the explosive hood jettison mechanism worked very well. At first we were apprehensive that the hood might be blown straight back and smash into the fin, but so far as I know this never happened. Once the hood was back far enough to break the aerodynamic lock, the airflow got underneath it and lifted it clear.

Once we had solved the problem of the canopy jettison system, I became interested in the idea of using similar explosive methods to eject the pilot from the FW190. Kurt Tank said he could not afford to divert the main design team to work on this, so in my own drawing office I drew out a design for such a seat and had it built. The seat was powered by a cartridge, but it soon became clear that this would not produce sufficient power to lift a man clear of the tail when the aircraft was moving at high speed. After about six months' work, which included ground firing

trials with a weighted dummy, it became clear that to get it to work such a seat would require far more effort than I could give it in addition to my duties as head of the prototype flight test department. So the idea was shelved. After the war I heard that Sir James Martin in Britain had perfected the design of a similar explosive ejector seat; but when I learned that it had taken several years of full-time work to get it to function properly, I did not feel too badly about my failure.

I regarded it as a point of honour that a test pilot should make every effort, even at risk to his life, to bring back his aircraft safely: a smoking heap of wreckage in a field was not only an expensive waste, but the fault that had caused the trouble might be concealed by the crash and the whole test programme could be set back as a result. To minimise the risks, I arranged my test flights so that if there was an engine failure I could usually glide back to the airfield. During the early part of the flight test programme engine failures were not all that uncommon and on more than one occasion this forethought stood me in good stead.

I never abandoned a Focke Wulf 190 in the air, though I must admit there were occasions when I came close to doing so. Once I was airborne in one of the early prototypes when suddenly there was a flash and the cockpit began to fill with dense and acrid smoke. I clamped on my mask and selected pure oxygen, then reduced speed and wound back the canopy. As a result I was able to breath, and see well enough to realise that the smoke was coming up from below my feet. Fire is the greatest hazard of all in an aircraft: if it reached the fuel tank under my seat, the chances of my survival would be

Left: Early in 1940 the new and more powerful BMW801 engine became available and was fitted into the V5 prototype in place of the smaller BMW139. It is believed that this photograph depicts the actual fitting of the BMW801 into the V5, in the experimental shop at Bremen.

Below left: The V5 depicted at about the time of its first flight, in April 1940. This aircraft still carries the smaller, more tapered wing, of the initial prototype aircraft./*VFW-Fokker*

slim. Many pilots, I know, would have got out there and then. Perhaps from a misplaced sense of professionalism, however, I carried on: as an engineer I was curious to know what was causing the trouble. It seemed like an electrical fire; if it was, and if it had not yet taken hold, the way to stop it was to remove the source of current. The only way to stop the generator with the electrical system as it then was, however, was to stop the engine. I feathered the propeller, shut the fuel cock and switched off the ignition. The engine came to a stop and, to my intense relief, the smoke began to die away. The FW190 was now a glider, but I had done a lot of flying in gliders so this posed no great problem. As usual I had conducted the trial with sufficient altitude to be able to glide back to the airfield in the event of an engine failure, and this was one of the occasions when this precaution paid off. My landing took everyone at the airfield by surprise: nobody heard me coming and the first thing they knew was when I was down. The landing was perfectly normal and the aircraft suffered no further damage. A subsequent examination revealed that the insulation had rubbed off some of the electrical wiring and the engine vibration caused an intermittent short circuit of the main 3 kilowatt electrical system; no wonder there had been a lot of smoke! After the incident

the electrical system was altered so that the generator could be switched out of circuit.

The first FW190 with the new BMW801 engine, the V5, flew in April 1940. The eighteen cylinder BMW801 was about 350 pounds heavier than the BMW139, which meant that a stronger mounting was necessary to support it. To compensate for this increased weight in the nose the fuselage had to be redesigned somewhat, with the cockpit moved back a little to keep the centre of gravity in the right place. This caused a slight deterioration in the pilot's field of vision forwards and downwards but it did confer one great bonus: since the engine and the cockpit were now further apart, at last one could fly in the new fighter without having one's feet gently roasted! With all the extra weight the wing loading shot up and the new versions did not handle so well as the earlier prototypes. To overcome this problem a re-designed wing of greater area was built.

In August 1940 I was flying in the V5 when it was involved in what could have been a nasty accident. I had not been up long when the access panel over the guns immediately in front of the cockpit started to come adrift. The panel was hinged at the rear and I knew that if the front fasteners let it go the airflow would get underneath it and the whole thing would slam back over my cockpit. I throttled

back and cut short the test, landing back at Bremen without first making my usual circuit of the airfield. I set down the aircraft normally and the panel remained in place; but as I was rolling to a halt there was suddenly an enormous crash and the next thing I knew I was upside down with the aircraft on top of me. Expecting the aircraft to burst into flames at any moment I frantically fought to get out and finally did so with some cuts and bruises. What had happened was that the ground staff had been using a quiet period to lay out some camouflage netting and I had collided with the trailer carrying it. The tractor driver had strict instructions not to drive on to the airfield but he had not expected me back so early and was keen to get the work completed before my arrival. Fortunately I had not been going fast at the moment of impact and the aircraft was not seriously damaged.

My task as test pilot had been to explore the safe operating limits of the FW190 and,

with the help of the design team, to bring the new fighter to the point where it would be accepted by the service authorities. As more and more pilots at the Rechlin test centre tried the aircraft, they became as enthusiastic as we were over its high performance and excellent handling characteristics. The FW190 was ordered into large-scale production.

Looking back, I believe that the fact that I was a qualified engineer as well as a test pilot did much to ease the passage of the FW190 into service and, later, through its development life. I think Kurt Tank agreed with this, because later he commented that he would not employ a test pilot who was not a qualified engineer. During the development phase it greatly speeded events when I was able to suggest workable engineering solutions to problems I had encountered in the air.

Reading the stories of aircraft which have proved successful, one often hears of how the test pilot jumped off the wing after the maiden flight and proclaimed to everyone that here

was a world-beating flying machine. Such statements might make nice copy for the firm's publicity people, but in my experience the reality of initial test flying is less theatrical. For the record, I never said any such thing after the maiden flight of the Focke Wulf 190. I am an engineer and during my training I had been taught to be cautious. After the first flight I told the members of the design team exactly what I had learned about the new fighter – which was not a great deal, since the flight had lasted only about half an hour. I said that so far as I had tried them the controls were light, positive and well-balanced, the trim was excellent and the aircraft had not demonstrated any vices; but about the fumes in the cockpit and the undercarriage up-lock . . .

Aircraft of the first production version of the FW190, the A-1, taken at Marienburg probably in July 1941. Included in this line-up are the 6th, 8th, 12th, 14th, 15th and 23rd aircraft of this series./*VFW-Fokker*

By the summer of 1941 the production of the FW190 was beginning to get into its stride. Between the beginning of July and the end of the year the Marienburg plant delivered a total of 133 of these aircraft to the Luftwaffe. The Arado plant at Warnemunde began production in August and produced a further 52, while the Ago plant at Oschersleben began in October and added 35 more. *Above left:* General view of one of the production lines for early series FW190s. *Left:* Lowering the BMW801 engine into place on an early production aircraft. *Above centre:* A test of the undercarriage retraction system; the FW190 was unusual amongst World War 2 fighters in having an electrical instead of a hydraulic retraction system. *Above right:* Final tuning of the engine. *Right:* Pre-flight walk-round by the production test pilot, prior to take-off./*VFW-Fokker*

Focke Wulf 190 in Service

Above and right: Cases of engines overheating were frequent, when the FW190 first went into service. These sometimes led to fires, as in the case of this foam-smothered A-1 belonging to II./JG 26. *Bundesarchiv*

Far right, top: In the field maintenance for an FW190A-1 of II./JG 26. One advantage of the electrically operated undercarriage was that by breaking the circuit to one of the legs, the other could be retracted for ground testing using a single external jack. *Bundesarchiv*

Far right, bottom: Ground crewmen man-handling off the airscrew of an FW190. The VDM constant-speed three-propeller had a blade diameter of 10ft 10in (3.3m), and weighed about 300lbs./*VFW-Fokker*

In the summer of 1941 the first FW190A-1s, the initial production version of the new fighter, began leaving the factory at Marienburg for the Luftwaffe. By the end of July 22 had been delivered to the service and the 6 Staffel of Jagdgeschwader 26, commanded by Oberleutnant Walter Schneider and based at Moorseele in Belgium, became the first operational unit to receive the new fighter. By the following September the whole of II./JG26, with a nominal strength of 30 aircraft, had been re-equipped and soon afterwards the FW190 went into action.

Some sources have suggested that the existence of a new type of fighter for the Luftwaffe was unknown to the Royal Air Force at this time, but this is not true. The Air Ministry Weekly Intelligence Summary dated 13 August 1941, a document issued to all Service units, stated:

'FW190 Fighter
A certain number of these new fighters have been produced, but information available is very scanty. The general design is said to be based on American practice and the aircraft is probably a low-wing monoplane with a fairly short fuselage and a span of about thirty feet. This new aircraft is fitted with a two-bank radial, an engine of the same type as that in the Dornier 217. It is definitely known that

this particular machine had to be fitted with an auxiliary mechanically-driven fan to keep the engine temperatures within reasonable limits. It is also reported that it is equipped with a very large airscrew and that the undercarriage is extraordinarily high in order to give the necessary ground clearance. Rough estimates show that the speed of the FW190 is somewhere between 370 and 380mph at 18-20,000ft.'

In general the report was accurate, except in two respects: firstly, the propeller fitted to the FW190 was not particularly large and its diameter and the overall height of the aircraft when sitting on the ground in the tail-down position compared closely with similar dimensions for the Spitfire; secondly, and far more important, the maximum speed of the FW190s now entering service had been underestimated by more than 30mph.

Soon afterwards combat reports began to mention a new German fighter. Following the action on 18 September in which the commander of II./JG26, Hauptmann Walter Adolph, was killed, an official RAF report noted the destruction of '. . . a Curtiss Hawk (or FW190) . . .' Three days later, after an action fought round escorted Blenheim bombers attacking the power station at Gusnay near Bethune, the Polish-manned No 315 Squadron reported that its Spitfires had destroyed '. . . one unknown enemy aircraft with a radial engine . . .' Almost certainly this was a reference to the FW190 flown by Leutnant Ulrich Dzialas of 8./JG26 who was shot down and killed that day.

The second *Gruppe* to re-equip with the FW190 was Major Gerhard Schoepfel's III./JG 26, which received its first aircraft in September 1941. *Below left:* In this photograph Schoepfel is seen leaving his personal aircraft. *Left:* Schoepfel's FW190 being pushed into a camouflaged hangar, probably at Coquelles near Calais. *Below centre:* In December 1941 Oberstleutnant Adolf Galland moved from the command of JG 26 to become *General der Jagdflieger.* Schoepfel assumed command of the whole *Geschwader* in his place and Hauptmann Josef 'Pips' Priller, depicted, took over III./JG 26. The 'S' and 'G' markings on Schoepfel's and Priller's aircraft were non-standard, as were the 'He' markings carried by this aircraft (*below*) of one of the *Stab* units of JG 26. *Bundesarchiv*

33

In spite of the slowly mounting evidence, some months were to pass before the RAF Intelligence staff would commit itself to a positive identification. The Weekly Intelligence Summary dated 29 October 1941 carried the passage:

'In recent weeks a radial-engined type of fighter has been encountered by the RAF and has been reported as a French aircraft, the Bloch 151, and as a new type of German fighter, the FW190. There is as yet insufficient evidence to say with certainty what the new aircraft is.'

During the months that followed production of the A-1 and A-2 versions of the new German fighter proceeded apace, with a total of more than two hundred delivered to the Luftwaffe by the end of the year. By then the British Intelligence service was able to confirm that the aircraft was in fact the Focke Wulf 190; it was also beginning to learn the disconcerting truth that the new German fighter could out-run, out-climb, out-dive and out-roll the Spitfire Mark V, the best aircraft RAF Fighter Command then had available. Kurt Tank's new radial-engined fighter began to present an uncomfortably sharp thorn in the side of the Royal Air Force, which was now committed to a policy of offensive sweeps over Belgium and northern France in an effort to tie down German units which might otherwise move to Russia.

The Royal Air Force's long term answer to the FW 190 was the Mark IX version of the Spitfire, fitted with an improved engine with two-stage supercharging. But the introduction of this aircraft would take time, and in the meantime Fighter Command would have to do the best it could with inferior equipment. How useful it would be if an example of the FW190 could be captured so that its weaknesses might be learned and, perhaps, exploited . . .

Left and right: Scramble take-off by aircraft of 7. Staffel of JG 2, probably from Morlaix in France in the summer of 1942./*Bundesarchiv*

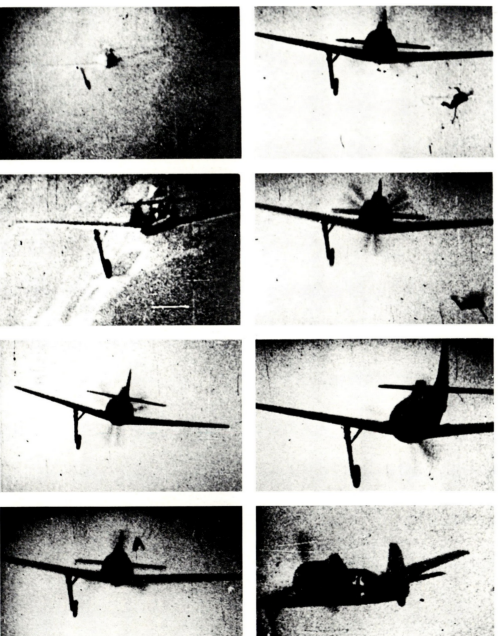

Left: Death of an FW190; although the FW190 had a better performance than the Mark V Spitfires confronting it on the Channel coast, the new German fighter was of course vulnerable to surprise attack. This remarkable series of photographs was taken by Flight Sergeant A. Robson, a New Zealander flying Spitfires with No 485 Squadron, during a combat near Ambletuese on the afternoon of 4 May 1942. Afterwards Robson reported:

"Flying as Blue 3 at 17,000ft I saw two FW190s 2,000ft below. Blue 1 dived to attack and I followed him. I fired two short bursts at one. He turned inland and I followed him to close range and fired the rest of my ammunition at him. I saw several hits. One wheel came down, the hood and pilot's helmet blew off. The enemy aircraft when last seen was flying with the starboard wing down at about 2,000ft". Robson, who obviously did not see the pilot baling out, afterwards claimed one enemy aircraft 'probably destroyed'. The FW190 almost certainly belonged to JG 2./*IWM*

Far left, bottom: In the spring of 1942 *JG 2* became the second *Geschwader* to re-equip with the FW190. Major 'Assi' Hahn commanded *III./JG 2;* the aircraft carries the markings of the *III. Gruppe* adjutant, and was probably used by Hahn as a reserve machine./*Bundesarchiv*

To Hijack a FockeWulf

'The art of war is divided between force and stratagem. What cannot be done by force must be done by stratagem.'

Frederick the Great

By the beginning of 1942 it was clear that the capture of an airworthy FW190 would be of inestimable value to RAF Fighter Command. Yet in wartime the acquisition of an example of the latest enemy fighter in an undamaged condition was a requirement far easier to state than to achieve. Nevertheless Captain Philip Pinckney, a Commando officer who was undeterred by the many obvious difficulties, put forward a proposal for two men to attempt to achieve by stealth what a battalion would not achieve by force: to steal one of the new German fighters and fly it back to England. For sheer effrontery the plan, which is reproduced in full below, can have few equals in military history. And it might just have succeeded.

MOST SECRET AND URGENT

To: Officer Commanding No 12 Commando
From: Captain Pinckney, E Troop, No 12 Commando

Sir,
I understand that as a matter of great urgency and importance a specimen Focke Wulf 190 is required in this country. I attach a proposal for procuring one of these aircraft.

I have the honour to request that this, my application to be allowed to undertake the operation described, may be forwarded as rapidly as possible through the correct channels to the Chief of Combined Operations I further propose that the pilot to accompany me should be Mr Jeffrey Quill who is a close friend of mine, and as a well known test pilot of fighter aircraft is well qualified to bring back the plane. He is also young, active, a yachtsman, and a man in every way suitable to carry out the preliminary approach by land and sea.

If Mr Quill cannot be allowed to undertake this operation, perhaps a substitute could be made available from the Free French Forces. I am most anxious to be allowed to volunteer for this operation.

I have the honour to be
    Sir
Your obedient servant
(signed) P H Pinckney

23.6.42

1 Object: to bring back to this country undamaged a Focke Wulf 190.

2 Forces Required:

One MGB (motor gunboat) equipped with DF (direction-finding radio) apparatus, to carry a folbot (collapsible canoe) to within two miles of the coast of France.

One folbot equipped with wireless transmitter.

One officer of a Commando.

One specially selected pilot.

Method

3 (Day 1)

a On the night of D1 the MGB, carrying the officers and folbot, will leave England after dark and proceed at best speed to within one or two miles of the French coast off a selected beach.

b On reaching the beach the folbot will be carried inland and hidden in a wood or buried in the dunes. The officers will lie up during the following day.

4 (Day 2)

After laying up all day the officers will move inland at nightfall until they are within observation range of a fighter aerodrome.

5 (Day 3)

a On D3 the officers will keep the aerodrome under observation and plan the attack for the start of nautical twilight (ie just before sunrise) on D4.

b During the night of D3 the officers will penetrate the aerodrome defences by stealth and will conceal themselves as near as possible to a selected Focke Wulf aircraft.

6 (Day 4)

a At the start of nautical twilight on D4, when the aircraft are warmed up by the ground mechanics, the two officers will take the first opportunity to shoot the ground mechanics of the selected plane as soon as it has been started up. The pilot officer will take off in the machine and return to England. The commando officer will first ensure the safe departure of the aircraft, and will then withdraw to a previously reconnoitred hideup. Should no opportunity to seize the aircraft have presented itself, the officers will withdraw to a hideup and make another attempt next morning.

b During the night of D4 the commando officer will return to the concealed folbot.

7 (Day 5)

a After nautical twilight of D5 or during the succeeding night, this officer will launch the folbot and be picked up by an MGB.

b The MGB should be off the coast for two hours before nautical twilight on D5, D6 or D7 providing the weather is calm. If the weather is unsuitable, the MGB should come on the first suitable morning. The officer after launching the folbot will paddle to a pre-arranged bearing. The MGB, making due allowance for the day and consequent set of the tide, will proceed on a course to intercept the folbot. In addition the officer will make wireless signals, which will be picked up by the MGB using DF gear.

Notes

8 Selected aerodrome

a The selection of an aerodrome will be dependent on intelligence not at present available to me. The requirements are:

1 Within 20 miles of a landing beach which is not too strongly defended, and which has a hinterland of dunes or woods offering a hiding place for the folbot.

2 Within observation range or a few miles of a covered approach or a wood or place of concealment.

b It is thought that possibly Abbeville aerodrome might be suitable with a landing made on the Somme estuary. The

Cherbourg Peninsula, entailing a cliff-climbing on landing, might give a good chance of making an undiscovered landing, providing a suitable aerodrome is nearby.

9 Return of the Plane: Arrangements must be made with Fighter Command to ensure that the pilot officer is not shot down by our fighters on returning with the captured aircraft. It is suggested that these arrangements should not be dependent upon wireless or on the officers taking distinctive markings or signalling apparatus with them. Possibly Fighter Command could be instructed not to shoot down any enemy Focke Wulf 190 appearing over the coast during specified times on selected days. In addition the undercarriage could be lowered for identification. If a Focke Wulf 190 after all is unprocurable on the aerodrome, a Messerschmitt 109F could be brought back instead. I understand that its aquisition would also be valuable.

10 Date: The landing should be made on a rising tide to cover footprints and also on a dark night to achieve suprise.

11 Alternative return of Commando officer. If it is considered an unacceptable naval risk to bring back an MGB to pick up the Commando officer, this officer could either paddle on a course pre-arranged by Fighter Command and eventually be picked up by an RAF rescue launch or, as a third alternative method of withdrawal, he could be instructed to make his way back through occupied France.

12 Other considerations:
a Food. The officers will be equipped with ten day's compressed rations.
b Preparation. The officers should have ample time to train together for a period which need not exceed ten days. Training should also be carried out on the MGB.
c Security. The officers suggested in the covering letter accompanying this proposal are both at present stationed at Bursledon, where they frequently go sailing together; the Commando officer owns a double folbot which is used daily; there are MGBs stationed at Bursledon; training could therefore be started without delay without arousing any suspicions that an operation was under rehearsal.

Pinckney's proposal was allocated the operational code-name 'Airthief' and detailed planning began; the airfield at Cherbourg-Maupertus was considered suitable for such an enterprise. Yet while still in the embryo stage 'Airthief' was overtaken by a coincidence more bizarre than any a fiction writer would devise. On the very evening after Pinckney submitted his paper, on 23 June 1942, a German pilot became disorientated during a

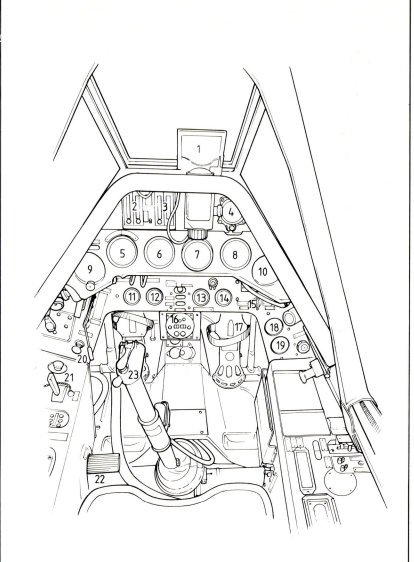

The cockpit of the FW190A-3.
Key:

1. Revi 16B reflector sight
2. and 3. Armament switches and round counters
4. FuG 16 ZY radio homing indicator
5. Airspeed Indicator
6. Artificial Horizon
7. Rate of climb/descent indicator
8. Repeater compass
9. Altimeter
10. Engine rpm gauge
11. Fuel and oil pressure gauge
12. Oil temperature gauge
13. Fuel contents gauge
14. Airscrew pitch indicator
15. Fuel guage selector switch
16. Bomb release control panel
17. Rudder pedal
18. Oxygen flow indicator
19. Oxygen pressure gauge
20. Landing gear up-lock release
21. Tailplane trim switch
22. Throttle
23. Control column, with gun firing button.

fight with Spitfires over southern England and inadvertently landed his FW190 at Pembrey in South Wales. So the RAF got its Focke Wulf, without having to resort to 'Airthief'.

Philip Pinckney did not survive the war; he was killed in action in Italy in 1944. Of the chances of success of 'Airthief', Jeffrey Quill recently commented:

'Provided we could get to the aircraft with its engine running, get the German airman out of the cockpit dead or alive and get me into it, I thought I had a 50-50 chance of getting back to England. As to the early part of the operation I was not qualified to have a view and I was guided entirely by Philip who seemed very confident and I would just have done what he said. He was obviously relying upon stealth – and perhaps we might have got away with it. Philip was always evasive about his own plans for getting back. I had a splendid way of getting back by air, but it was a very different kettle of fish for him. But he was very resourceful and might well have made it, one way or another, provided I had got the aircraft off the airfield without too much of a hue and cry.

'Anyway, it was a non-event, as it turned out. Philip Pinckney was the inspiration behind the whole thing. Had it succeeded it would have been 90 per cent due to him and the balance of danger would have been heavily against him. I think he was bitterly disappointed when it was called off and he was quite cross about the German pilot landing in Wales. I am afraid I have to confess to a certain easing of tension within my guts!'

Unsolicited Testimonials

'Captured Focke Wulf 190 will be flying in Green Area from 29/6 onwards from RAE Farnborough with or without Spitfire escort. All aircrews and gunners are to be warned that attacks should not, repeat, not, be made on FW190 aircraft in this area. FW190 will carry British markings.' Secret teleprinter message from Headquarters Fighter Command to air defence units, 29 June 1942.

The chance acquisition of the Focke Wulf 190 sent a ripple of excitement running through Fighter Command. Plans were laid to examine the aircraft in the minutest detail, both in the air and on the ground, in an effort to learn everything possible about it. Such an investigation takes time, however, and while it was in progress the Commander in Chief of Fighter Command, Air Chief Marshal Sir William Sholto Douglas, felt it necessary to write a strongly worded letter about the FW190 to the Under Secretary of State for Air, Lord Sherwood.

MOST SECRET

Headquarters, Fighter Command
Royal Air Force
Bentley Priory
Stanmore
Middlesex

FC/S. 29470
17th July, 1942

Sir,

I attach a memorandum on the performance and operational characteristics of day fighters, with particular reference to what our position will be in the Spring of 1943 (not reproduced here). I ask that immediate consideration should be given to the points raised in this memorandum.

1 It is scarcely necessary for me to emphasise the point that quality is more important than quantity in the production of fighters. At the beginning of the war our

Below: The captured FW190A-3, works number 313, pictured in the markings of its new owners.

fighters possessed technical superiority over those of the enemy. We have gradually lost this lead and we are now in a position of inferiority. It is essential that this position should be remedied before next spring, when it is anticipated that intensive air fighting will take place.

2   I seem to detect a spirit of complacency in the Ministry of Aircraft Production. This is borne out by the speeches of the Minister of Production and the Minister of Aircraft Production in the debate in the House of Commons on Tuesday, 14 July. They appear to find it difficult to believe that we have really lost our lead in fighter performance. There is however no doubt in my mind, nor in the minds of my fighter pilots, that *the FW190 is the best all-round fighter in the world to-day.* (Author's italics.) It is no answer to say that the position will

be reversed when the Spitfire IX comes into general use. In the first place I have only fourteen Spitfire IXs, whereas the enemy has between two and three hundred FW190s. In several respects the FW190 is superior to the Spitfire IX, eg in climb and acceleration at certain critical altitudes and in negative G carburation. The most alarming aspect of the position however is that, whereas the Spitfire with the Merlin engine is almost at the end of its possible development, the FW190 is only in the early stages of its development. Reports are already to hand of more horsepower being put into the engine of the FW190, and there is no doubt that with its greater engine capacity, it can in time easily outstrip the Merlin Spitfire in performance. This in fact is likely to have happened by next Spring.

3   In my opinion therefore this is no time for complacency in regard to the quality and performance of our day fighter aircraft. In the attached memorandum will be found certain suggestions for making the necessary improvements. These are the result of a study of the problem by my technical staff, who may not have all the facts and future possibilities at their fingertips. At the same time I ask that they should be given serious consideration.

I have the honour to be,

Sir,

Your obedient Servant,

(signed)   W S Douglas
Air Chief Marshal
Air Officer Commanding-in-Chief
Fighter Command, Royal Air Force

The under Secretary of State
Air Ministry,
Whitehall, S.W.1

Time would show that Sir Sholto Douglas had taken a pessimistic view; he had overestimated the ability of improved versions of the FW190 to '. . . outstrip the Merlin Spitfire in performance.' In fact the Spitfire IX and its successors would prove worthy opponents for the contemporary versions of the FW190. Nevertheless the letter does show, in no uncertain terms, the concern the German fighter caused in the Royal Air Force.

Following the initial flight trials at the Royal Aircraft Establishment at Farnborough, in July 1942 the captured Focke Wulf 190 was sent to the Air Fighting Development Unit at Duxford for tactical trials. The resultant report, issued in August 1942 and reproduced below almost in its entirety, is a model of what such an intelligence document should contain. The aircraft described was the FW190A-3. In places the language used is complimentary in the extreme. The reader

should bear in mind that these are not the words of a Focke Wulf salesman trying to boost his firm's product, but those of one forced to give grudging admiration in wartime to the product of an enemy.

BRIEF DESCRIPTION OF THE AIRCRAFT
The FW190 is a small, compact, single-seater, single-engined, low wing monoplane fighter. There are fittings under the fuselage to enable it to carry bombs or a jettisonable fuel tank. It has a fully retractable undercarriage and partially retractable tailwheel. The mainplane is fully cantilever and is fitted with split flaps of metal construction. The flaps have four positions: retracted, 15° for take-off, 30° for use in the event of a baulked landing, and fully down for landing. Operation is by means of three electric push buttons.

The power unit is a BMW801-D, 14-cylinder, 2-row radial engine, fitted with a two-speed supercharger giving the best performance at 9,000 and 18,000ft. Between 5,000 and 8,000ft the performance of the engine falls off as it is just below the height where the two-speed supercharger comes into operation. The estimated power of the engine is 1,700hp at the maximum power altitude of 18,000ft. The engine oil coolers and induction system are totally enclosed by an extremely neat cowling and cooling is assisted by an engine driven fan behind the propeller.

The constant speed VDM 3-bladed metal propeller is electrically operated. It is automatically controlled by an hydraulic governor and if required manually, by an electric switch on the pilot's throttle lever.

The undercarriage is retracted by pushing a red button. The operation for lowering the undercarriage consists of pushing a green button and releasing the undercarriage locks by pulling a lever which is situated on the left-hand side of the cockpit. In the event of an electrical failure, the only emergency method of lowering the undercarriage is by means of this lever, gravity completing the operation. The tailwheel is partially retracted, and lowered, mechanically by a cable attached to the starboard undercarriage leg. It is fully castoring and can be locked for take-off and landing by holding the control column right back.

All the control surfaces are fabric covered and are fitted with metal trimming tabs which can be adjusted only on the ground. For trimming, the tailplane is adjustable in flight over the range of +5° to −3°. It is operated electrically by two push buttons governing the up and down movements. There is a visual indicator in the cockpit.

The armament consists of 4 x 20mm guns

in the wing and 2 x 7.92mm machine guns in the engine cowling. The all-up weight of the aircraft, including pilot, is approximately 8,600lb and the wing loading is 41.8lb sqft.

Pilot's Cockpit

The cockpit is fully enclosed and although rather narrow is otherwise extremely comfortable. The pilot's position is excellent and as his feet are level with the seat, it enables him to withstand high acceleration forces without 'blacking-out'. The positioning of instruments is excellent and all controls fall easily to the pilot's hand, the absence of unnecessary levers and gadgets being particularly noticeable. The front panel is in two pieces, the top containing the primary flying and engine instruments and the lower panel the secondary instruments. Cut-out switches for the electrical circuits are housed in hinged flaps on the starboard side.

The switches and indicators for the operation of the undercarriage, flaps and tail incidence, are situated on the port side. The control column is the standard German fighter type with a selector switch and firing button for guns, and a send/receive button for the wireless.

The cockpit canopy, which is made of moulded plexiglas, is well shaped and extends far back along the fuselage. The bullet-proof windscreen has a pronounced slope which is unusual. The canopy can be slid back for entry and exit and for taxi-ing, operation being by means of a crank handle similar to that in the Westland Whirlwind. The enclosure can be jettisoned in an emergency by pressing a red lever on the starboard side; this unlocks the hood and detonates a cartridge which breaks the runners and blows the canopy off. Heating for the cockpit appears efficient, and cooling is effected by a small flap on the port side and seems quite sufficient for the pilot's comfort.

Armour Plate

The pilot's bucket seat is made of 8mm armour plate and in the unprotected gaps behind are fitted shaped strips varying in thickness between 5 and 6mm. The pilot's head and shoulders are protected by shaped armour plate 13mm thick and the windscreen is of bullet-proof glass about $1\frac{3}{4}$in thick. Both fuel tanks are self-sealing. The oil tank, which is situated in front of the engine cowling, is protected by a ring of armour plate varying in thickness, and the tank itself is surrounded by a toughened steel ring.

Radio

The wireless installation is the old type FuG7 and the only unusual feature is that there is no wireless mast, there being instead a short aerial between the tail fin and the cockpit canopy.

Oxygen

The aircraft is fitted with standard improved *Hohenatmer* oxygen equipment with *Blaser* attachment, giving pure oxygen at high altitude. Three bottles of unusual shape are the source of supply. It was not possible to test the efficiency of this equipment but it is understood that the RAE are carrying out investigations and will render a report in due course.

Compass

A Patin Distant Reading Pilot's Compass is installed in the centre of the dashboard and the Master Unit is in the rear of the fuselage. An aircraft silhouette takes the place of the normal needle and indicates the direction which the aircraft is flying. There is an adjustable verge ring which can be set to any desired course and the aircraft then turned until the silhouette is pointing to the course selected. The compass generally is of excellent design and the dial is situated in a position where it can be easily seen by the pilot. The magnet is many times more powerful than in our compasses, and as a result is less affected by northerly turning and acceleration errors. It is also unaffected by current or voltage fluctuations, or changes in temperature.

ARMAMENT CHARACTERISTICS

The armament consists of:—

i   Two MG17 guns of 7.92mm calibre fitted above the engine, synchronised, firing through the propeller arc.
ii Two MG151/20 guns of 20mm calibre, synchronised, firing through the propeller arc are installed in the wing roots about 12in out from the engine cowling.
iii Two Oerlikon FF20mm guns fitted in the wings outboard of the propeller arc.

Gun Buttons and Switches

The guns are fired by means of a button on the front of the control column. A small selector switch at the side of the column enables the pilot to select the following alternatives:—

i   MG17 and MG151/20 guns.
ii Oerlikon FF20mm guns.
iii All guns.

In addition to this it is possible, by means of cut-out switches, which are situated on the starboard side of the cockpit, to fire each pair of guns independently. There are ammunition counters in the cockpit for each gun.

Heating

Hot air from the engine cowling is led by means of ducts to the ammunition chutes of the MG17 guns and thence upwards to the breech mechanism. The Oerlikon FF20mm guns are also heated by hot air from the engine cowling. No special provision is made for heating the MG151/20 guns and it is thought that owing to their position near the engine this is unnecessary.

Sight

A reflector sight, type Revi 12-D, is mounted 1½in to starboard of the vertical centre line. The graticule is 5° 48′ in diameter, which is the equivalent to approximately 95mph for the high muzzle velocity of the German armament. Vertical and horizontal lines are marked off in degree steps from the centre of the graticule. Seven such lines are visible each way, these lines assist the pilot in range estimation and allowing for line.

Harmonisation

The harmonisation ranges for each pair of guns are:—

Two MG17 guns at 300 metres or 330 yards
Two MG151/20 guns at 450 metres or 490 yards
Two Oerlikon FF20mm guns at 250 metres or 270 yards.

The gun lines of the MG17 guns are not symmetrical about the vertical centre line. The port gun converges whereas the starboard gun diverges with the result that they cross over 1ft 2in to starboard. This may be due to incorrect harmonisation.

Sighting View

The sighting view, when sitting comfortably in the normal position, is about half a ring (of deflection) better than that from a Spitfire. The view downwards from the centre of the sight graticule to the edge of the reflector plate holder, is about 5 degrees. This view is not obtained by elevating the guns (and consequently the sight) relative to the line of flight, but is entirely due to the attitude of the aircraft in flight, which is nose down.

TACTICAL TRIALS

General

The FW190 is considered an excellent low and medium altitude fighter. It is fast, well armed and very manoeuvrable. The fighting qualities have been compared with a Spitfire VB, Spitfire IX, Mustang IA, Lockheed P-38F, Typhoon and the prototype Griffon engined Spitfire. All aircraft were carrying full war load.

Flying Charactetristcs

The aircraft is pleasant to fly, all controls being extremely light and positive. The aircraft is difficult to taxi due to the excessive weight on the self-centring tailwheel when on the ground. For take-off, 15° of flap is required, and it is necessary to keep the control column back to avoid swinging during the initial stage of the take-off run. The run is approximately the same as that of the Spitfire IX.

Once airborne, the pilot immediately feels at home in the aircraft. The retraction of the flaps and undercarriage is barely noticeable although the aircraft will sink if the retraction of the flaps is made before a reasonably high airspeed has been obtained.

The stalling speed of the aircraft is high, being approximately 110mph with the undercarriage and flaps retracted, and 105mph with the undercarriage and flaps fully down. All controls are effective up to the stall. One excellent feature of this aircraft is that it is seldom necessary to re-trim under all conditions of flight.

The best approach speed for landing with flaps and undercarriage down is between 130 and 140mph Indicated, reducing to about 125mph when crossing the edge of the aerodrome. Owing to the steep angle of glide, the view during the approach is good and the actual landing is straightforward, the touchdown occurring at approximately 110mph. The landing run is about the same as that of the Spitfire IX. The view on landing is poor due to the tail-down attitude of the aircraft. The locking of the tailwheel again assists in preventing swing during the landing run.

The aircraft is very pleasant for aerobatics, even at high speed.

Performance

The all-round performance of the FW190 is good. Only brief performance tests have been carried out and the figures obtained give a maximum speed of approximately 390mph True, at 1.42 atmospheres boost, 2,700rpm at the maximum power altitude of about 18,000ft. All flights at maximum power were carried out for a duration of 2 minutes only.

There are indications that the engine of this aircraft is de-rated, this being supported by the pilot's instruction card found in the cockpit. Further performance tests and engine investigation are to be carried out by the RAE and more definite information will then be available.

Throughout the trials the engine has been running very roughly and as a result pilots flying the aircraft have had little confidence in its reliability. The cause of this roughness has not yet been ascertained but it is thought that it may be due to a bad period of vibration at certain engine speeds which may also affect the injection system. (This roughness was later found to be due to fouling of the Bosch sparking plugs after short periods of running; the fault was cleared by fitting Siemens type plugs taken from the BMW801A engine of a crashed Do217 bomber—Author).

Endurance

The total of 115 gallons of fuel is carried in two self-sealing tanks and each tank is fitted with an immersed fuel pump for use at altitude. A total of 9 gallons of oil is carried in a protected oil tank. The approximate endurance under operational conditions, including dog-fights and a climb to 25,000ft is approximately 1 hour 20 minutes. There is a red warning light fitted in a prominent position which illuminates when there is only sufficient fuel left for 20 minutes flying.

Climb

The rate of climb up to 18,000ft under maximum continuous climbing conditions at 1.35 atmospheres boost, 2,450rpm, 165mph is between 3,000 and 3,250ft/min. The initial rate of climb when pulling up from level flight at fast cruising speed is high and the angle steep, and from a dive is phenomenal. It is considered that the de-rated version of the FW190 is unlikely to be met above

25,000ft as the power of the engine starts falling off at 22,000ft and by 25,000ft has fallen off considerably. It is not possible to give the rate of climb at this altitude.

Dive

The FW190 has a high rate of dive, the initial acceleration being excellent. The maximum speed so far obtained in a dive is 580mph True, at 16,000ft, and at this speed the controls, although slightly heavier, are still remarkably light. One very good feature is that no alteration of trim from level flight is required either during the entry or during the pull-out. Due to the fuel injection system it is possible to enter the dive by pushing the control column forward without the engine cutting.

Search View

The view for search from the FW190 is the best that has yet been seen by this Unit. The cockpit hood is of moulded plexiglas and offers an unrestricted view all round. No rear view mirror is fitted and it is considered unnecessary as the backward view is so good. The hood must not be opened in flight as it is understood that tail buffeting may occur and that there is a chance of the hood being blown off. This, however, is not a disadvantage for day search as the quality of the

Below: Close-up of the canopy of the captured FW190. Royal Air Force officers were greatly impressed by the visibility from the pilot's position and the official report compiled by the Air Fighting Development Unit stated: 'The view for search from the FW190 is the best that has yet been seen by this unit.'

plexiglas is excellent. During conditions of bad visibility and rain, or in the event of oil being thrown on the windscreen, the fact that the hood must not be opened in flight is obviously a disadvantage.

Instrument Flying

The aircraft, although extremely light on all controls, is reasonably easy to fly on instruments. There are no artificial horizon or climb and dive indicators, which are naturally missed by British pilots. It appears that instrument flying is carried out by use of the gyro compass, turn and bank indicator, altimeter and air speed indicator.

Low Flying

The good all-round view from the aircraft, particularly over the nose, makes the FW190 very suitable for low flying and ground strafing. Another good point is that the sight is depressed, which would probably help in preventing pilots from flying into the ground. In conditions of bad visibility, however, low flying is likely to be unpleasant as the hood must not be opened in flight.

Formation Flying

The aircraft is easy to fly in formation and due to the good view, all types of formation can be flown without difficulty. The aircraft has a wide speed range which greatly assists in regaining formation, but care must be taken to avoid over-shooting as its clean lines make deceleration slow.

Night Flying

The aircraft was not flown at night but was inspected with the engine running on a dark night, with no moon. The cockpit lighting appeared very efficient and did not reflect on the canopy. The exhaust flames viewed from about 100 yards ahead were seen as a dull red halo, and viewed from the beam could be seen from about 500 yards away. The flame can be seen from astern about 200 yards away. It is considered that the glare will badly affect the pilot, particularly during take-off and landing. Although the aircraft carried full night flying equipment, there is no indication that flame dampers are normally fitted. It is possible that the cause of the red flame may be due to faulty mixture.

Engine Starting and Quick Take-Offs

It is possible to start the engine by means of the internal battery, or an external battery, and in the event of emergency by hand. The method of starting is similar to the ME109, being an inertia system. If the engine is cold it will require running for a considerable time before the oil temperature reaches the safety level for take-off and even with a warm engine some minutes are necessary as the cooling is so effective on the ground. This is obviously a disadvantage and coupled with the fact that the aircraft is not easy to taxi, makes the FW190 inferior to our aircraft for quick take-offs.

Fighting Qualities

The fighting qualities of the FW190 have been compared with various aircraft, and each comparison is dealt with separately. The trials against the Griffon Spitfire were only tried and against the Typhoon had to be abandoned before completion owing to the unsatisfactory state of the engine of the FW190.

FW190 versus Spitfire VB

The FW190 was compared with a Spitfire VB from an operational squadron for speed and all-round manoeuvrability at heights up to 25,000ft. The FW190 is superior in speed at all heights, and the approximate differences are as follows:—

At 1,000ft the FW190 is 25-30mph faster than the Spitfire VB

At 3,000ft the FW190 is 30-35mph faster than the Spitfire VB

At 5,000ft the FW190 is 25mph faster than the Spitfire VB

At 9,000ft the FW190 is 25-30mph faster than the Spitfire VB

At 15,000ft the FW190 is 20mph faster than the Spitfire VB

At 18,000ft the FW190 is 20mph faster than the Spitfire VB

At 21,000ft the FW190 is 25mph faster than the Spitfire VB

At 25,000ft the FW190 is 20-25mph faster than the Spitfire VB

Climb

The climb of the FW190 is superior to that of the Spitfire VB at all heights. The best speeds for climbing are approximately the same, but the angle of the FW190 is considerably steeper. Under maximum continuous climbing conditions the climb of the FW190 is about 450ft/min better up to 25,000ft. With both aircraft flying at high cruising speed and then pulling up into a climb, the superior climb of the FW190 is even more marked. When both aircraft are pulled up into a climb from a dive, the FW190 draws away very rapidly and the pilot of the Spitfire has no hope of catching it.

Dive

Comparative dives between the two aircraft have shown that the FW190 can leave the Spitfire with ease, particularly during the initial stages.

Manoeuvrability

The manoeuvrability of the FW190 is better than that of the Spitfire VB except in turning circles, when the Spitfire can quite easily out-turn it. The FW190 has better acceleration under all conditions of flight and this must obviously be useful during combat.

When the FW190 was in a turn and was attacked by the Spitfire, the superior rate of roll enabled it to flick into a diving turn in the opposite direction. The pilot of the Spitfire found great difficulty in following this manoeuvre and even when prepared for it was seldom able to allow the correct deflection. A dive from this manoeuvre enabled the FW190 to draw away from the Spitfire which was then forced to break off the attack.

Several flights were carried out to ascertain the best evasive manoeuvres to adopt if 'bounced'. It was found that if the Spitfire was cruising at low speed and was 'bounced' by the FW190, it was easily caught even if the FW190 was sighted when well out of range, and the Spitfire was then forced to take avoiding action by using its superiority in turning circles. If on the other hand the Spitfire was flying at maximum continuous cruising and was 'bounced' under the same conditions, it had a reasonable chance of avoiding being caught by opening the throttle and going into a *shallow* dive, provided the FW190 was seen in time. This forced the FW190 into a stern chase and although it eventually caught the Spitfire, it took some time and as a result was drawn a considerable distance away from its base. This is a particularly useful method of evasion for the Spitfire if it is 'bounced' when returning from a sweep. This manoeuvre has been carried out during recent operations and has been successful on several occasions.

If the Spitfire VB is 'bounced' it is thought unwise to evade by diving steeply, as the FW190 will have little difficulty in catching up owing to its superiority in the dive.

The above trials have shown that the Spitfire VB must cruise at high speed when in an area where enemy fighters can be expected. It will, then, in addition to lessening the chances of being successfully 'bounced', have a better chance of catching the FW190, particularly if it has the advantage of surprise.

FW190 versus Spitfire IX

The Focke Wulf 190 was compared with a fully operational Spitfire IX for speed and manoeuvrability at heights up to 25,000ft. The Spitfire IX at most heights is slightly superior in speed to the FW190 and the approximate differences in speeds at various heights are as follows:—

At 2,000ft the FW190 is 7-8mph faster than the Spitfire IX

At 5,000ft the FW190 and the Spitfire IX are approximately the same

At 8,000ft the Spitfire IX is 8mph faster than the FW190

At 15,000ft the Spitfire IX is 5mph faster than the FW190

At 18,000ft the FW190 is 3mph faster than the Spitfire IX

At 21,000ft the FW190 and the Spitfire IX are approximately the same.

At 25,000ft the Spitfire IX is 5-7mph faster than the FW190

Climb

During comparative climbs at various heights up to 23,000ft, with both aircraft flying under maximum continuous climbing conditions, little difference was found between the two aircraft although on the whole the Spitfire IX was slightly better. Above 22,000ft the climb of the FW190 is falling off rapidly, whereas the climb of the Spitfire IX is increasing. When both aircraft were flying a high cruising speed and were pulled up into a climb from level flight, the FW190 had a slight advantage in the initial stages of the climb due to its better acceleration. This superiority was slightly increased when both aircraft were pulled up into the climb from the dive.

It must be appreciated that the differences between the two aircraft are only slight and that in actual combat the advantage in climb will be with the aircraft that has the initiative.

Dive

The FW190 is faster than the Spitfire IX in a dive, particularly during the initial stage. This superiority is not so marked as with the Spitfire VB.

Manoeuvrability

The FW190 is more manoeuvrable than the Spitfire IX except in turning circles, when it is out-turned without difficulty.

The superior rate of roll of the FW190 enabled it to avoid the Spitfire IX if attacked when in a turn by flicking over into a diving turn in the opposite direction, and as with the Spitfire VB, the Spitfire IX had great difficulty in following this manoeuvre. It would have been easier for the Spitfire IX to follow the FW190 in a diving turn if its engine had been fitted with a negative 'g' carburettor, as this type of engine with the ordinary carburettor cuts very easily.

The Spitfire IX's worst heights for fighting the FW190 are between 18,000 and 22,000ft and below 3,000ft. At these heights the FW190 is a little faster.

Both aircraft 'bounced' one another in order to ascertain the best evasive tactics to adopt. The Spitfire IX could not be caught when 'bounced' if it was crusing at high speed and saw the FW190 when well out of range. When the Spitfire IX was cruising at low speed its inferiority in acceleration gave the FW190 a reasonable chance of catching it up and the same applied if the position was reversed and the FW190 was 'bounced' by the Spitfire IX, except that overtaking took a little longer.

The initial acceleration of the FW190 is better than the Spitfire IX under all conditions of flight, except in level flight at such altitudes where the Spitfire has a speed advantage and then, providing the Spitfire is cruising at high speed, there is little to choose between the two aircraft.

The general impression gained by pilots taking part in the trials is that the Spitfire IX compares favourably with the FW190 and that provided the Spitfire has the initiative, it has undoubtedly a good chance of shooting the FW190 down.

FW190 versus Mustang 1A (P-51A)

The FW190 was compared with a fully operational Mustang IA for speed and all-round performance up to 23,000ft. There was little to choose between the aircraft in speed at all heights except between 10,000 and 15,000ft, where the Mustang was appreciably faster. Approximate differences were as follows:

> At 2,000ft the FW190 is 2mph faster than the Mustang IA
> At 5,000ft the Mustang is 5mph faster than the FW190
> At 10,000ft the Mustang is 15mph faster than the FW190
> At 20,000ft the FW190 is 5mph faster than the Mustang IA
> At 23,000ft the FW190 is 5mph faster than the Mustang IA

Climb

The climb of the FW190 is superior to that of the Mustang IA at all heights. The best climbing speed for the Mustang is approximately 10mph slower than that for the FW190; the angle is not nearly so steep and the rate of climb is considerably inferior. When both aircraft are pulled up into a climb after a fast dive, the inferiority in the initial stage of the climb is not so marked, but if the climb is continued the FW190 draws away rapidly.

Dive

Comparative dives have shown that there is little to choose between the two aircraft and if anything the Mustang is slightly faster in a prolonged dive.

Manoeuvrability

The manoeuvrability of the FW190 is better than that of the Mustang except in turning circles where the Mustang is superior. In the rolling plane at high speed the Mustang compares more favourably with the FW190 than does the Spitfire.

The acceleration of the FW190 under all conditions of flight is slightly better than that of the Mustang and this becomes more marked when both aircraft are cruising at low speed.

When the FW190 was attacked by the Mustang in a turn, the usual manoeuvre of flicking into a diving turn in the opposite direction was not so effective against the Mustang as against the Spitfire, particularly if the aircraft were flying at high speed. The fact that the engine of the Mustang does not cut during the application of negative 'g' proved a great asset and gave the Mustang a reasonable chance of following the FW190 and shooting it down. It must be appreciated, however, that much depends on which aircraft has the initiative and that obviously the FW190 can escape if the Mustang is seen well out of range. The FW190 in this case will almost certainly utilise its superior climb.

Trials were carried out to ascertain the best manoeuvre to adopt when 'bounced'. If the Mustang was cruising at high speed and saw the FW190 about 2,000 yards away, it usually managed to avoid by opening up to full throttle and diving away, and once speed had been built up it was almost impossible for the FW190 to catch it. When the Mustang was 'bounced' by the FW190 when flying slowly, it was unable to get away by diving and was forced to evade by means of a quick turn as the FW190 came into firing range.

When the FW190 was 'bounced' by the Mustang, it could evade by using its superiority in the rolling plane and then pull up violently from the resultant dive into a steep climb which left the Mustang behind. If the Mustang is not seen until it is fairly close, it will get the chance of a short burst before it is out-climbed.

Against the FW190 the worst heights for the Mustang IA were above 20,000ft and below 3,000ft where the FW190 is slightly superior in speed. The best height for the Mustang was found to be between 5,000 and 15,000ft.

FW190 versus Lockheed P-38F Lightning

The FW190 was compared with an operationally equipped P-38F flown by an experienced US Army Air Force pilot. The two aircraft were compared for speed and all-round manoeuvrability at heights up to 23,000ft. The FW190 was superior in speed at all heights up to 22,000ft where the two aircraft were approximately the same. The difference in speed decreases as the P-38F gains altitude, until at 23,000ft it is slightly faster. The approximate differences in speeds are as follows:

At 2,000ft the FW190 is 15mph faster than the P-38F

At 8,000ft the FW190 is 15mph faster than the P-38F

At 15,000ft the FW190 is 5-8mph faster than the P-38F

At 23,000ft the P-38F is 6-8mph faster than the FW190

Climb
The climb of the P-38F is not as good as that of the FW190 up to 15,000ft. Above this height the climb of the P-38F improves rapidly until at 20,000ft it becomes superior. The best climbing speed for the P-38F is about 20mph less than that of the FW190 and the angle approximately the same. The initial rate of climb of the FW190 either from level flight or a dive is superior to that of the P-38F at all heights below 20,000ft, and above this height the climb of the P-38F becomes increasingly better.

Dive
Comparative dives between the two aircraft proved the FW190 to be better, particularly in the initial stage. During prolonged dives the P-38F on occasion was catching up slightly with the FW190, but during actual combat it is unlikely that the P-38F would have time to catch up before having to break off the attack.

Manoeuvrability
The manoeuvrability of the FW190 is superior to that of the P-38F, particularly in the rolling plane. Although at high speed the FW190 is superior in turning circles, it can be out-turned if the P-38F reduces its speed to about 140mph, at which speed it can carry out a very tight turn which the FW190 cannot follow.

The acceleration of the two aircraft was compared and the FW190 was found to be better in all respects.

When the FW190 'bounced' the P-38F and was seen when over 1,000 yards away, the pilot's best manoeuvre was to go into a diving turn and if it found the FW190 was catching it up, to pull up into a spiral climb, flying at its lowest possible speed. Although time did not permit trials to be carried out with the FW190 being 'bounced' by the P-38F, it is thought that the P-38F would stand a reasonable chance of shooting down the FW190 provided it had a slight height advantage and the element of surprise. If the

pilot of the FW190 sees the P-38F when it is just out of range, a quick turn in one direction followed by a diving turn in the opposite direction will give the P-38F a most difficult target, and as the acceleration and speed of the FW190 in a dive builds up very rapidly, it is likely to be able to dive away out of range.

FW190 versus 4-cannon Typhoon
Owing to the unsatisfactory condition of the engine of the FW190 which caused the trials to be abandoned, only brief tests could be carried out against the Typhoon. Arrangements have been made with the RAE Farnborough to complete the trials as soon as the engine of the FW190 has been overhauled and passed fit for further flights. Trials were carried out against two operationally equipped Typhoons, one from a squadron and the other from the Hawker Aircraft Company. Both aircraft were flown by experienced pilots.

The FW190 was compared with the Typhoon for speed and all-round manoeuvrability at 2,000ft and in addition a partial climb was carried out between 12,000 and 17,000ft. At 2,000ft there was little to choose between the two aircraft, the Typhoon being slightly faster. The runs were made from cruising speed at full throttle for a period of two minutes and this did not give the Typhoon time to build up to its maximum speed. From the knowledge of both aircraft it can be safely assumed that the Typhoon will be faster than the FW190 at all heights, having the best advantage in speed at the following approximate heights: 8,000ft, 10,000ft, 16,300ft and 20,500ft.

Climb
During the partial climb from 12,000 to 17,000ft, the Typhoon was out-climbed by the FW190 quite easily. The best climbing speed of the Typhoon is considerably higher than that of the FW190 and the angle not nearly so steep, the rate of climb at all heights being inferior. The difference in a comparative climb after a dive is unlikely to be so great.

Dive
It is thought that the Typhoon will out-dive the FW190, but the FW190 is likely to be slightly better in the initial stage. The controls of the Typhoon, although good in a dive, are not so light and responsive as those of the FW190.

Manoeuvrability
The manoeuvrability of the FW190 and the Typhoon was compared during one flight at 2,000ft, the Typhoon being flown by a very experienced test pilot from Hawkers, and it appeared that there was little to

choose between the two aircraft in turning circles. The opinion of both pilots was that it was doubtful whether either aircraft would be able to hold its sights on sufficiently long for accurate sighting. It should be borne in mind, however, that the pilot of the FW190 was reluctant at the time to risk stalling the aircraft in the turn at such a low height, and it is therefore possible that the turn could have been made tighter. The Typhoon was unable to follow the FW190 from a turn in one direction into a diving turn in the opposite direction due to the FW190's superiority in the rolling plane. The initial acceleration of the Typhoon, particularly from slow speed, is much slower although the difference is acceleration when flying at high speed is not so great. It is considered that the FW190 would have the greatest difficulty in 'bouncing' the Typhoon provided the Typhoon was flying at high speed. The Typhoon, however, should have a good chance of 'bouncing' the FW190 provided it has a slight height advantage.

FW190 versus Griffon Spitfire (went into service as the Spitfire XII)
Two brief flights at between 1,000 and 2,000ft were carried out between the FW190 and the prototype Griffon Spitfire flown by an experienced test pilot from Messrs Vickers. Two speed runs were made from high cruising speed over a distance of about 10 miles. The acceleration of the Spitfire proved superior to that of the FW190 and its speed appreciably faster. Owing to adverse weather conditions it was not possible to compare the two aircraft for dive and climb.

Manoeuvrability
Brief manoeuvrability tests were carried out and the Spitfire had no difficulty in out-turning the FW190. It again should be borne in mind, however, that the pilot of the FW190 was reluctant at the time to risk stalling the aircraft in the turn at such a low height and it is therefore possible that the turn could have been tighter and the difference between them less marked.

CONCLUSIONS
The FW190 is undoubtedly a formidable low and medium altitude fighter.

Its designer has obviously given much thought to the pilot. The cockpit is extremely well laid out and the absence of large levers and unnecessary gadgets is most noticeable. The pilot is given a comfortable seating position, and is well protected by armour.

The simplicity of the aircraft as a whole is an excellent feature, and enables new pilots to be thoroughly conversant with all controls in a very brief period.

The rough running of the engine is much disliked by all pilots and must be a great disadvantage, as lack of confidence in an engine makes flying over bad country or water most unpleasant.

The armament is good and well positioned, and the ammunition capacity should be sufficient for any normal fighter operation. The sighting view is approximately half a ring (of deflection) better than that from the Spitfire.

The all-round search view is the best that has yet been seen from any aircraft flown by this unit.

The flying characteristics are exceptional and a pilot new to the type feels at home within the first few minutes of flight. The controls are light and well harmonised and all manoeuvres can be carried out without difficulty at all speeds. The fact that the FW190 does not require re-trimming under all conditions of flight is a particularly good point. The initial acceleration is very good and is particularly noticeable in the initial stages of a climb or dive. Perhaps one of the most outstanding qualities of this aircraft is the remarkable aileron control. It is possible to change from a turn in one direction to a turn in the opposite direction with incredible speed, and when viewed from another aircraft the change appears just as if a flick half-roll has been made.

It is considered that night flying would be unpleasant, particularly for landing and take-off, due to the exhaust glare and the fact that the cockpit canopy cannot be opened in flight.

The engine is easy to start but requires running up for a considerable time, even when warm, before the oil temperature reaches the safety level for take-off, and this coupled with the fact that the aircraft is not easy to taxi makes the FW190 inferior to our aircraft for quick take-offs.

The comparative fighting qualities of the FW190 have been compared with the Spitfire VB, Spitfire IX, Mustang IA, Lockheed P-38F, 4-cannon Typhoon and prototype Griffon Spitfire, all aircraft being flown by experienced pilots. The main conclusion gained from the tactical trials of the FW190 is that our fighter aircraft must fly at high speed when in an area where the FW190 is likely to be met. This will give our pilots the chance of 'bouncing' and catching the FW190 and, if 'bounced' themselves, the best chance of avoiding being shot down.

The all-round search view from the FW190 being exceptionally good makes it rather difficult to achieve the element of surprise. Here again, however, the advantage of our aircraft flying at high speed must not be overlooked, as they may even if seen by the pilot of the FW190 catch it before it has time to dive away.

In Defence of the Reich

American heavy bombers made their first attack on a target in Germany itself, on Wilhelmshaven, on 27 January 1943. At that time Jagdgeschwader 1 was the sole home defence day fighter *Geschwader* and its *Stab* and II., III., and IV. Gruppen were wholely or partially equipped with the FW190. The unit's Focke Wulfs often carried unusual markings. *Right:* A black and white checker-board cowling, with the marking of 2. Staffel. *Below:* A face marking painted on an FW190 of II. Gruppe. *Far right, top:* 'FW190 and Nutcracker' badge, believed to belong to a *Stab* unit of JG 1.

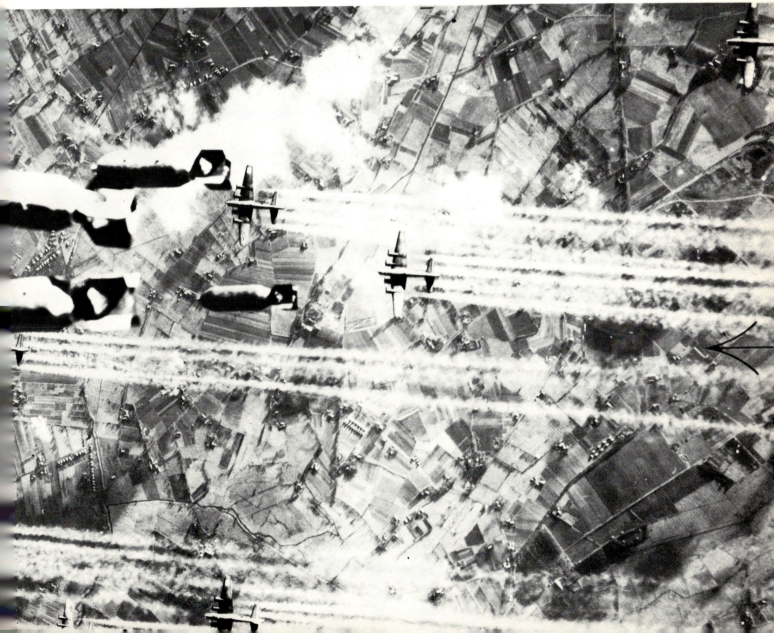

Below: Striking back at the tormentors: bombs falling away from B-17 Fortresses on 26 April 1943, when 107 of these heavy bombers attacked the Focke Wulf works at Bremen. Jagdgeschwader 1 fought a ferocious battle with the raiders and shot down fifteen bombers for a loss of five fighters shot down and five more damaged. *USAF*

The appearance of the strongly-built American heavy bombers over Germany led to demands for more-powerfully armed fighters for the home defence units. Amongst the armament combinations tried out in combat were *Right:* six 20mm cannon and *Far right:* two 30mm MK103 weapons in place of the outer-wing 20mm guns./*VFW-Fokker*

Below: An FW190, believed to be an aircraft of JG 1, attacking a Fortress of the 95th Bomb Group during the attack on Bremen on 29 November 1943. *USAF*

Left: It was from massive concrete operations bunkers like this one at Arnhem/Deelen, the command post of Jagd-division 3, that the German fighter forces were controlled during the hard-fought day and night battles from the middle of 1943.

Below left: No photograph can adequately convey the sense of bustle and drama within a command post when the battle was being fought, but this artist's impression comes close. The layout varied slightly from bunker to bunker, but all were similar to a cinema with the main situation map in place of the screen. In this example the Chief Operations Officer (1) sat near the rear of the 'stalls', with his broadcast officer on his right; in front of them sat the fighter liaison officers in telephone contact with the fighter airfields. Plots on the positions of the bombers and the defending fighters were flashed onto the air situation map on the right of the picture.

During the latter part of 1943 FW190s began operating against American daylight bomber formations with a new weapon, the Wgr 21 rocket. This improvised weapon comprised a 21cm spin-stabilised infantry mortar rocket, fired from a simple tube launcher. The weight of the rocket at launch was 248lbs (111kg), of which 90lbs (41kg) was warhead. In action the two wing-mounted rockets were fired simultaneously, using the B-2 button mounted on the control stick./*via Creek*

Focke Wulf 190
Rocket Firer

Right: Groundcrew fitting the launching tube to the wing supporting hook. The carrier strut, which attached the launcher to the hook, carried an electrically primed explosive charge to sever the strut if the pilot wished to jettison the launcher./*Bundesarchiv*

Left: Fitting the time fuse to a Wgr 21, prior to loading. The fuse exploded the missile after a pre-set flight time usually corresponding to a flight time of about 1,000 yards. In action, however, the Wgr 21 proved disappointing. It was extremely difficult for the pilot of the launching aircraft to judge the range accurately enough so that the rockets detonated within lethal range (about 30 yards) of the target; the great majority of these missiles exploded harmlessly either short of the bombers or past them. *Bundesarchiv*

Top left: Groundcrew lowering a rocket into the launching tube./*Bundesarchiv*

Centre left: Final adjustment of the bracing struts, which were lengthened until the launcher was held firmly in place. *Bundesarchiv*

Below: FW190s of II./JG 3, seen carrying a single Wgr 21 launcher under the fuselage. These rockets were in fact fired *rearwards*, as a final parting shot at the bombers as the fighters overtook them after attacks with their forwards-firing cannon. This use of rockets was not successful, however, and saw little use./*via Girbig*

Focke Wulf 190 Night Fighter

In the summer of 1943 Royal Air Force night bombers successfully used aluminium foil, code-named 'Window', to jam out the German night fighters' airborne and ground control radars. As a temporary expedient Focke Wulf 190 and Messerschmitt 109 fighters, seeking their prey visually without the use of radar, were pressed into action in the night air defence role under the code-name *Wilde Sau* (Wild Boar)./*VFW-Fokker*

Above: The architect of the *Wilde Sau* tactics was Major Hajo Herrmann, pictured here with Hermann Goering during an inspection of pilots. *Herrmann*

Above right: Since initially the *Wilde Sau* pilots lacked radar, they had to rely on searchlights to illuminate night bombers for them so that they could attack. If there was a layer of cloud over the target the searchlight crews would adopt *Mattscheibe* (ground glass screen) tactics, playing their beams on the base of the clouds so that the light diffused and silhouetted bombers flying above. The success of this method is shown in this photograph, taken looking down on a Lancaster flying over Berlin on the night of 16 December 1943./*IWM*

Right, Far right, top: Early in 1944 a few FW190s were fitted with *Neptun* radar, to enable them to seek out bombers on their own. This particular aircraft, seen with its pilot Oberleutnant Krause, belonged to the operational trials unit Nachtjagdgeschwader 10 based at Werneuchen near Berlin and was used on operations during the summer of 1944. The transmitter aerials were fitted to the rear fuselage, the left/right receiver aerials were fitted above each wing and the above/below receiver aerials were fitted just in front of the cockpit and under the starboard wing, respectively. On the nose of the aircraft can be seen the *Wilde Sau* badge, a boar's head. *Bundesarchiv*

Centre left: Cockpit of a night fighting FW190, showing the cathode-ray tube for the *Neptun* radar just under the top coaming.

Below: Alternative aerial scheme for the *Neptun* radar, fitted to some FW190s.

Mediterranean Jabo
Adolf Dilg

A fast and sturdy aircraft, it was only a matter of time before the FW190 was impressed into service in the Jabo (fighter-bomber) role. The first such *Gruppe* to be fully equipped with the type was III./ZG2; Adolf Dilg served on the unit and this is his story.

In August 1942 the III.Gruppe of Zerstoer-ergeschwader 2, with which I was serving as a *Feldwebel* pilot, was withdrawn to Parndorf near Vienna to re-equip with the Focke Wulf 190A-4; we were to be the first *Jabo Gruppe* to receive a full complement of this aircraft.

We found the FW190 a great improvement over the Messerschmitt 109E we had been using over Russia. For the Jabo role is was better in every respect: it was much faster, it handled better, it was more rugged and easier to maintain in the field and it was much more stable on the ground especially when it had a bomb on board.

The conversion training lasted about a month then, in September, we moved to Cognac near Bordeaux in France for special-ised training in anti-shipping operations. For some time it had been clear that the Allies were building up forces for amphibious assault operations and our unit was one of those in the Luftwaffe assigned to the counter-invasion role. In the mouth of the Gironde an old French destroyer lay aground and against her we practised low level and dive bombing attacks using 550 and 1,100lb cement training bombs. We also received some practical training in penetrating the Bordeaux balloon barrage, which proved an exciting business.

In October some of the more experienced pilots in the *Gruppe*, myself included, were ordered to the operational airfield at Merville near Lille. There we joined the *Jabo Staffeln* of JG2 and JG26 and took part in a large scale attack on Canterbury, a reprisal for those being made by the RAF against German cities. Following this action, the whole *Gruppe* was transferred to Comiso in Sicily.

We had not been there long when, on 8 November 1942, Allied troops landed in Algeria and Morocco and we received orders to move with the utmost possible speed to

Tunisia. At last we were to go into action in our designated 'counter-invasion' role. Almost from the moment we arrived at Sidi Ahmed near Bizerta, we were in the thick of the fighting. On 12 November Allied troops captured Bone and the town became their main supply port for the advance into Tunisia. We went into action against shipping off the port but a nasty shock awaited us: the ships put up a veritable wall of flak and in addition we had to face large numbers of enemy fighters. It soon became clear that in this theatre Jabo operations were going to be far more hazardous than they had been in Russia.

On 2 December we lost our *Gruppe Kommandeur*, Hauptmann Wilhelm Hachfeld, nicknamed 'Bomben Willi' because of his success as a Jabo pilot. It was one of those silly accidents well clear of the enemy, which have claimed so many aces. He had just begun his take-off run for an attack on an enemy position when he collided with a Messerschmitt 109 from another airfield which had just landed and stopped on the runway. Hachfeld's Focke Wulf nosed over on to its back and caught fire, and he was dead before the rescue team could get him out. From outside our crew room we watched with horror as the drama unfolded, unable to do anything to help.

Soon the Allies began to mount bombing attacks on our airfield, though initially with little effect. Our air defence fighters, Messerschmitt 109s of I. and II./JG53 and FW190s from II./JG2, dealt severely with several of the early bombing attacks. (During one of the

attacks on Sidi Ahmed, on 4 December, No 18 Squadron of the RAF lost all eleven of the Bisley bombers which took part. *Author*.)

As well as maintaining the pressure on the shipping around Bone and attacking enemy artillery positions, supply dumps and vehicles near the front line, we also bombed the airfields at Thelepte, Tebessa and Kairouan. Towards the end of December our *Gruppe* was re-designated III./Schnellkampfgeschwader 10 (the third *Gruppe* of Fast Bomber Geschwader 10). The change made no difference to our operations; these continued exactly as before.

Most of our attacks were straightforward, though on a few occasions we had to plan attacks on two or three different targets then wait at *Sitzbereitschaft* (cockpit readiness) in our bombed-up aircraft until a last-minute decision on which one we were to go for. This happened if we had to synchronise our attack with one by the army, or if an enemy attack was expected and we were to provide support for our troops when it was launched.

Gradually the German and Italian forces in Tunisia were squeezed tighter and tighter, as the Allies closed in on us from both the east and the west. In the air we faced overwhelming enemy forces and the pace of operations was such that our losses began to mount disastrously. Throughout my time in North Africa there was no shortage of aircraft, fuel or bombs; but we received very few replacements for the pilots we lost. And the pilots we did get often straight from training and,

lacking experience, did not survive for very long; all too often one would arrive from Sicily in the late afternoon and be killed in action during the next couple of days. Things went from bad to worse until at one stage we had no officers left in the *Gruppe* and attacks were being led by a *Feldwebel*. In January the fighter-bomber ace Oberleutnant Fritz Schroeter arrived to take command of the *Gruppe*, but by then things had moved beyond the point where individuals could do much to alter the course of events.

Clearly the end was near for the German and Italian forces in Africa, though I was not to see it personally. On 24 January 1943 I was part of a patrol flying cover for a naval convoy bringing in supplies from Italy. We had just been relieved and I was on my way home when suddenly I saw tracer going past my aircraft; there was a series of bangs, then my Focke Wulf shuddered and burst into flames. We had been 'bounced' out of the sun by American Lightnings. I rolled the aircraft on to its back, jettisoned the canopy and baled out. As I was coming down the shock of the encounter began to wear off and I could feel a severe pain in my left forearm. I looked down and my blood ran cold as I caught sight of my flying suit cut to ribbons and my arm bleeding profusely. A cannon shell had passed clean through my arm, shattering the bone. By the time I hit the water I had lost the use of my right arm altogether. With some difficulty I managed to inflate my life jacket, but my dinghy resisted all attempts to get it to blow up using only one hand. I spent a couple of hours in the water in intense pain then, to my great good fortune, an Italian destroyer hove into view and came almost straight towards me. My distress flares caught the crew's attention and I was picked up. The destroyer took me back to Tunisia, then a few days later I was moved to Italy with other wounded.

The injuries to my arm were so severe that initially the Army doctors were all set to amputate it at the elbow. Again I was lucky, however, because the Luftwaffe medical people got to hear about it and I was whisked away to one of their hospitals where the conditions were much better. There doctors were able to graft a piece of bone from my leg and so saved my arm. My recovery was so complete that, in October 1943, I was passed as fit for flying again.

I returned to III./SKG10, which was then re-forming at Graz in Austria following the heavy losses it had suffered during the fighting in the Mediterranean area in the spring and summer. Soon after my return, however, it became clear that although the Luftwaffe doctors had done a fine job my repaired arm was not strong enough for operational flying. My career as a Jabo pilot was over.

Top left: FW190 fighter-bombers flying in the three aircraft *Kette* formation employed by ground attack units./*Bundesarchiv*

Bottom left: Close up of the bomb fusing selector panel, fitted in the FW190 beneath the centre of the instrument panel. The electrical bomb fusing system enabled the pilot to select the type of fusing he wanted at any time prior to release, which gave him the advantage of flexibility. The simple pointer-switch could be set to safe (*Aus*), for diving (*Sturz*) or Horizontal (*Wagerecht*) attacks, with delayed fusing (*mit Verzoegerung* – MV) or without it (*ohne Verzoegerung* – OV). A longer delay fusing was required for low altitude horizontal attacks than for dive attacks. Lights fitted immediately above the fusing panel, to a maximum of four, came on to show when the bombs on the various carriers had been released. *VFW-Fokker*

Top right: 'Rechlin' type dive bombing attack employed by the FW190:

1. Aircraft approached the target to one side, throttled back, as pilot or formation leader assessed wind drift. Altitude about 2,500m (about 8,000ft).
2. As target disappeared beneath the wing, the aircraft was banked into the dive.
3. Once in the 50 degree dive the speed built up rapidly, sometimes reaching 800kph (500mph) at the bomb release point.
4. At an altitude of 1,200m (about 4,000ft) the nose was eased up 3 degrees and one second later . . .
5. . . . the bomb was released. Immediately after release the pilot began the pull out, at the same time turning to avoid enemy ground fire.
6. Descending to about 50m (about 150ft) the fighter-bomber made its getaway.

Centre right: Typical approach for a low-altitude attack by FW190 fighter-bombers, flying with 80-100 yards between aircraft and 150-200 yards between *Schwaerme.* Leader would take the formation to an easily identified point to one side of the target, then turn in for a *Steckrubenwerf* attack with his aircraft following in line astern.

Bottom right : Steckrubenwerf (turnip-lob) low altitude bombing attack:

1. Approach at an altitude of about 50m (about 150ft) at a speed of about 500kph (310mph).
2. About one mile from the target the pilot eased up the nose of his aircraft . . .
3. . . . leveled off at about 300m (about 1,000ft) and lined up on the target before going into a shallow descent.
4. He held the target in the centre of his sight.
5. One second before bomb release the nose was eased up 3 degrees (to ensure that the bomb cleared the propeller), then the bomb was released.
6. Evasive turn and getaway.

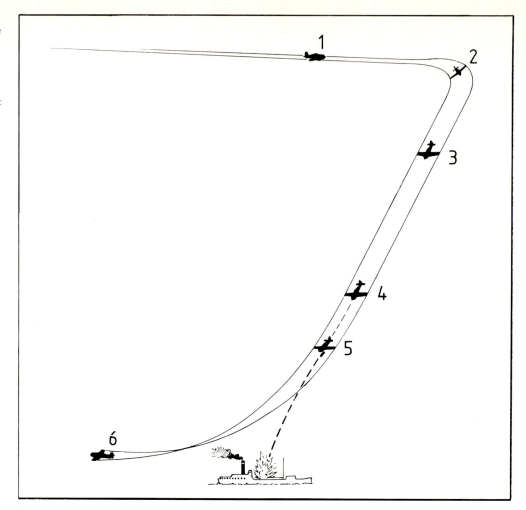

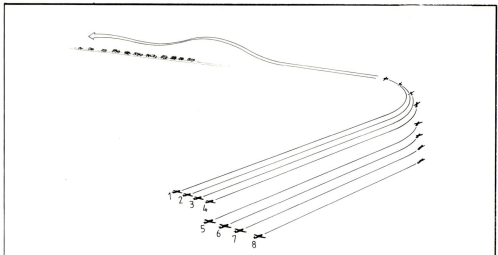

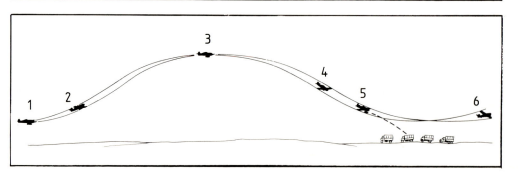

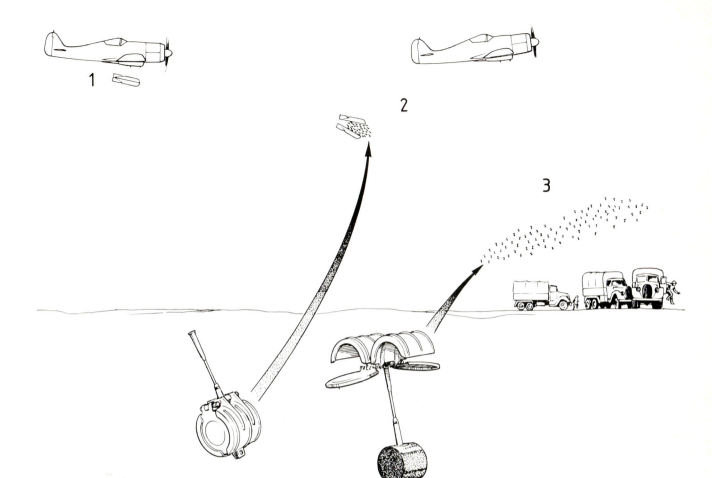

Above: Steckrubenwerf attack with an AB-250-3 small bomb container:

1. Aircraft releases AB-250-3 container.
2. When safely clear of the aircraft the container opens longitudinally and 108 SD-2 bomblets, still closed, fall clear.
3. The SD-2s' wings open, arming the bombs, and they flutter to the ground.

Left: Groundcrew loading an AB250 small bomb container on the fuselage bomb release slip of an FW190./*Bundesarchiv*

Oberfaehnrich, later Leutnant, Helmut Wenk of the IV. Ergaenzungs (training) Gruppe of Schnellkampfgeschwader 10, pictured with his aircraft at Cognac in France in May 1943. The aircraft was an A-4./*Wenk*

Above: Wenk went into action with II./SKG 10 against the Allied forces in Sicily in July 1943. This photograph shows the unit's operations post, situated under a cork tree just off the airfield at Crotone. From left to right: Ofw Rehwoldt, unidentified (not a pilot), Ofw Rippelsieb (on telephone), Leutnant Klein, Uffz Thrun, unidentified armourer./*Wenk*

Right: A close shave for Helmut Wenk on 27 July 1943. Due to the ever-present risk of air attack, take-offs were made in rapid succession from Crotone. On this occasion Wenk was blinded by the dust kicked up by the aircraft in front and he struck a tree to one side of the airstrip. The aircraft careered away, shedding both wings, both drop tanks, both undercarriage legs and, fortunately, the bomb. The Focke Wulf finally came to rest half way down the sloping runway overshoot, bearing a shaken but otherwise uninjured pilot./*Wenk*

Left: Helmut Wenk taking off from Crotone on 1 August 1943, to attack the Allied munitions dump at Nicosia in Sicily. His aircraft carried two 65 gallon drop tanks and one 550lb bomb and was one of eight engaged in the attack. The raiders dive-bombed the dump, setting it on fire, then returned at low altitude along the road from Nicosia to Taormina shooting up supply vehicles. Wenk shot up an armoured vehicle and two lorries, before falling foul of a mobile anti-aircraft gun which scored three hits on his aircraft; he succeeded in getting back to Crotone and making a normal landing but the aircraft never flew again. Two of the fighter-bombers failed to return from this mission./*Wenk*

Below: The route flown by the aircraft of 6. Staffel of SKG 10 during the attack on Nicosia on 1 August 1943.

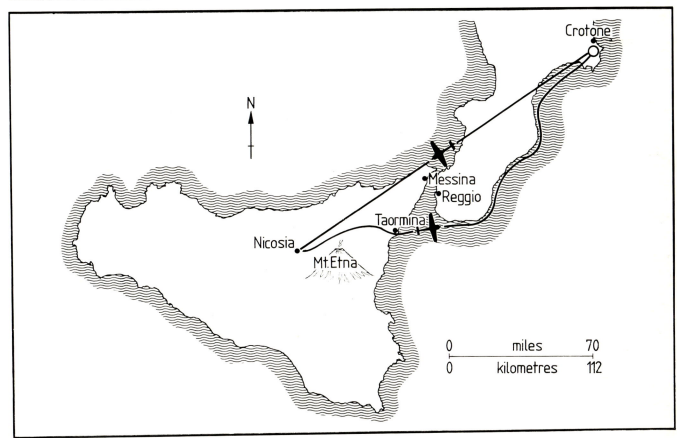

FW190s of SKG10 pictured during the hard-fought battles in Italy in the autumn and winter of 1943. *Left:* Armourers preparing to lift a 550lb bomb on to one of the aircraft. *Centre left:* With ground crewmen on the wing to guide the pilot to the take-off point, an FW190 laden with an 1,100lb bomb moves out of its dispersal point. *Bottom left:* At the beginning of the take-off run. *Below:* A formation of FW190s moving out for an attack. *Right:* A dive-attack with a 1,100lb bomb.

The battles round the Allied lodgement area at Anzio were some of the hardest-fought of the war, with the German ground-attack units heavily committed. *Top left:* This picture shows the close-support air command post of Luftflotte 2 during the Anzio battle, situated in slit trenches overlooking the Allied bridgehead. Present, from left to right, Oberleutnant Kluge, Generalfeldmarschall Baron Wolfram von Richthofen (cousin of the World War 1 fighter ace) the commander of Luftflotte 2, General von Pohl, Oberst Christ. *Centre left:* General view of the command post, with von Richthofen on the far right examining the bridgehead through binoculars. Von Richthofen was the leading German exponent of close-support air operations and frequently took personal command of the air battle. *Below:* View out to sea from von Richthofen's command post, showing Allied shipping burning off the coast. *via Rigelsford*

Right: A *Staffel* of ground attack FW190s, believed to belong to SKG 10, photographed at Deplin-Irena near Warsaw where it was engaged in training./*via Heise*

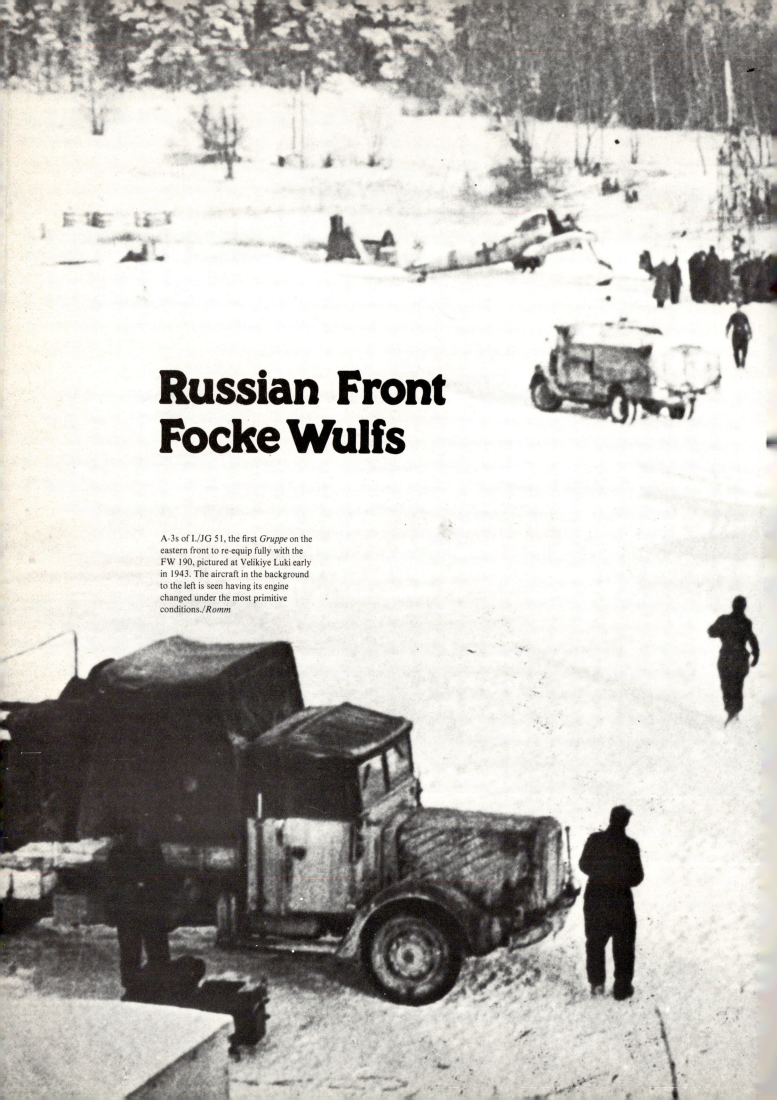

Russian Front Focke Wulfs

A-3s of I./JG 51, the first *Gruppe* on the eastern front to re-equip fully with the FW 190, pictured at Velikiye Luki early in 1943. The aircraft in the background to the left is seen having its engine changed under the most primitive conditions./*Romm*

Left: FW190 A-3 of III./JG 51.

Below: This A-5, also of III./JG 51, was wrecked after a crash landing near Tschemlysch on the central part of the front in August 1943./*via Girbig*

Right: An A-4 of I. Gruppe of Jagdgeschwader 54, with an 1,100lb SC500 bomb under the fuselage, about to taxi out of its log-covered dispersal point in Russia./*via Redemann*

This page, top right: FW190A-4s of I. Gruppe of JG 54, pictured operating from Siwerskaja near Leningrad in the winter of 1943-1944./Bundesarchiv

Right: The Zwerg (dwarf) petrol fired hot air engine heater, an important piece of equipment if fighters were to be held at readiness during the harsh Russian winter. VFW-Fokker

Far left: Major 'Sepp' Wurmheller, credited with a total of 102 victories of which 93 were in the West. He commanded first the 9. Staffel of JG 2, later the III. Gruppe. He was killed on 22 June 1944 during a dogfight over France, when he collided with his wing man./*Bundesarchiv*

Left: Major Anton Hackl served on all the major war fronts and was credited with a total of 192 victories, of which 87 were in the West; he himself was shot down eight times, but survived the war. Amongst the units he commanded were III./JG 11, II./JG 26, Jagdgeschwader 300 and Jagdgeschwader 11. *Bundesarchiv*

Below: Oberleutnant Adolf Glunz spent most of his career with II./JG 26 and was credited with 71 victories, all but three of which were in the west. He survived the war./*via Girbig*

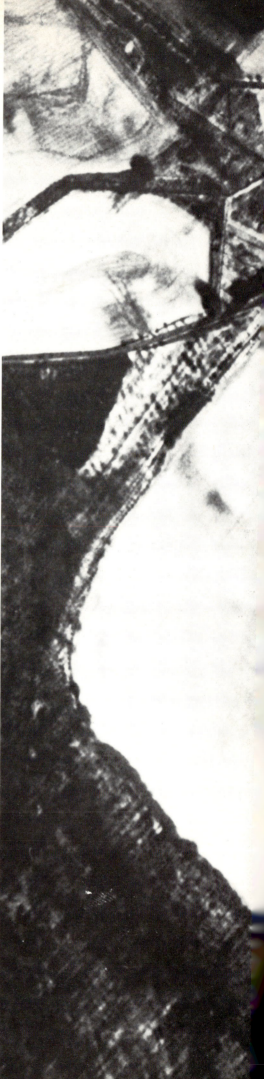

Above: Major Heinz Baer, the commander of II./JG 1, pictured with the B-17 Fortress he shot down on 22 February 1944; behind Baer stands his wing man Oberfeldwebel Leo Schuhmacher. Baer later commanded Jagdgeschwader 3 and ended the war credited with 220 victories of which 79 were in the West and 45 were in the Mediterranean area. He survived the war, but was killed in a light plane crash in 1957. *Bundesarchiv*

Right: Baer's combat report, 29.4.1944.

Far right: An FW190 dives in to finish off a B-17 Fortress which had already been hit and forced to leave the formation, immediately following the attack on the Focke Wulf factory at Oschersleben on 11 January 1944. During this action the US 8th Air Force lost a total of 60 heavy bombers, one of the heaviest losses of the war./*USAF*

Baer, Major   Operational Headquarters
II./Jagdgeschwader 1   1 May 1944
—Stab—

Combat Report on the Shooting-Down of a Thunderbolt on 29.4.44 – 10.56 hours in Map Reference HB by Major Baer, Stab II./JG 1 FW190 – "red 13"

On 29.4.44, after being at cockpit readiness, I took off at 09.40 hours with the Gruppe. The orders were to join up with I./JG 1 and III./JG 1 over Paderborn and head in the direction of Kassel climbing to an altitude of 7,000m. We were then vectored on to a heading of 130 degrees and after further corrections sighted the enemy in the area of Hanover. Near Brunswick we engaged Boeings and Liberators heading eastwards with a very strong fighter escort. Following a head-on attack, during which I shot down a Liberator, our formation was split up by the strong fighter escort and a series of combats developed between aircraft in twos and fours. I pulled up sharply and saw beneath me an FW190 with its right undercarriage leg extended being chased by a Thunderbolt. I immediately positioned myself behind the Thunderbolt and opened fire from the rear and above from a distance of about 150 metres, whereupon the Thunderbolt blew up and the pieces fell vertically to the ground. The wreckage hit the ground to the south of Brunswick.

Date and Time of
Victory: 29.4.44 – 10.56 hours

Position of Victory: HB – south of Brunswick

Altitude: 7500m

Witness: Ofw. Schuhmacher.

No Place for a Beginner
Fritz Buchholz

'In no other profession are the penalties for employing untrained personnel so appalling or so irrevocable as in the military.'
General Douglas MacArthur

During the summer of 1944 the serious losses suffered by the single-engined fighter units on all fronts led to a massive influx of pilots from other parts of the Luftwaffe, hastily retrained to fill the gaps in the ranks. Fritz Buchholz, previously a twin-engined fighter pilot, received only the sketchiest training in flying the FW190 before he was thrown into the battle. Outnumbered by enemy fighters whose pilots had had a considerably better training, an air combat could have only one result.

I held the rank of *Feldwebel*, when I joined my first operational flying unit at the end of 1943: the II Gruppe of Zerstoerergeschwader 26.

Flying the twin-engined Messerschmitt 410 heavy fighter, we operated against the American heavy bomber formations over eastern Germany and during the late spring I shot down two Liberators using my 5cm cannon. As the enemy escort fighters began to range deeper and deeper over our homeland, however, our Gruppe and others similarly equipped began to suffer severe losses while our success rate against the bombers declined.

It soon became clear that under such conditions there was little future for the Me410 as a bomber destroyer and, in July 1944, we received orders to convert on to the Focke Wulf 190; for the conversion we remained at our airfield at Koenigsberg/Oder. As the new aircraft arrived our Gruppe was redesignated as the II. Gruppe of Jagdgeschwader 6 and we were told that we were to operate in an

Below: FW190s hidden in a wood, beside a forward landing ground in France./*Bundesarchiv*

Left: Feldwebel Fritz Buchholz, thrown into action with II./JG 6 which had hastily converted from the Me410 to the FW190, had to learn the hard way that an air battle was no place to learn how to handle a single seat fighter./*Buchholz*

Below: Fritz Buchholz's FW190, No 21, pictured at Koenigsburg/Oder during the rapid conversion of II./JG 6 on to the type. Note the full-sized B-17 painted on the hangar doors, to assist pilots in judging the range of this aircraft when engaging it with the 5cm cannon carried by the Me410./*Buchholz*

entirely new role: that of air superiority fighter and ground attack. For the latter the aircraft were fitted with launchers for 21cm rockets, in addition to the normal armament of four 20mm cannon and two 13mm machine guns.

On 3 August 1944 I made my first flight in the FW190. I found the aircraft pleasant to fly, though after the excellent ground visibility of the Me410 the massive motor cowling of the Focke Wulf was disconcertingly restrictive. Flying against the heavy bombers in the Me410 had been rather like driving one truck against another; fighter-versus-fighter combat in a FW190 was something quite different. This might not have been so bad, had there been sufficient time for us to assimilate our new role. But this was not the case. The battle round the allied bridgeheads in Normandy was entering its most critical phase and we were to go into action as soon as possible. On 18 August, just over two weeks later and with 10 hours 54 minutes flying time in the FW190, I received orders to depart with the *Gruppe* for France on the following day.

Flying in easy stages, we took four days to move ourselves and our forty-odd brand-new FW190A-8s from Koenigsberg to our forward operational base at Herpy near Reims. At that time the Allied air superiority was such that the permanent Luftwaffe bases in France were all being bombed regularly. So the operational units were forced to move out and use im-

Left: Oberstleutnant 'Pips' Priller, the Kommodore of JG 26, being helped out of his aircraft during the battle of France in the summer of 1944. The location is believed to be the field landing ground either near Rambouillet or Chaumont-en-Vexin, both of which were used by Stab/JG 26 at this time. Priller survived the war credited with a total of 101 victories, all in the West. *Bundesarchiv*

Above: Following each operation the German fighters had to be carefully concealed, to prevent their landing grounds being found by the omni-present Allied reconnaissance aircraft. *Bundesarchiv*

provised airstrips in the surrounding country-side; the move had been planned before the invasion, and the fields surveyed and stocked with the necessary fuel and ammunition. Our airstrip at Herpy was nothing more than a piece of flat cow pasture surrounded by trees in which our aircraft could be hidden; nearby was our tented accommodation. The Allied fighter-bombers seemed to be everywhere and our survival depended on the strictest attention to camouflage. As part of this we even had a herd of cows which were moved on to the airfield when no flying was in progress. As well as giving the place a rustic look, these performed the valuable task of obliterating the tracks made on the grass by the aircraft. Such attention to detail paid off and there were no attacks on Herpy while I was there.

On the day after my arrival at Herpy, 23 August, I made three flights getting to know the local area; and one more on the 24th. On none of these flights did I come into contact with the enemy, though some members of the *Gruppe* did. Although our small pasture was excellent from the point of view of camouflage, the confined space did make it difficult for the unit to get airborne rapidly. During our first day there two aircraft collided during take-off, probably because one of them had run into the turbulent slipstream from the pair that had taken-off immediately ahead.

When we arrived at Herpy the German retreat out of Normandy was in its closing stages; the troops were streaming back across the Seine, making frantic demands for air cover to give them some respite from the incessant Allied air attacks. Since we were to operate as fighters rather than as ground-attack aircraft, the hefty 21cm rocket launchers were removed from our aircraft.

On the third day after our arrival in France, 25 August, we took off for our first full-scale operation: a sweep by the entire *Gruppe* as far as the Seine or as directed by our ground controller when we were airborne. Led by our *Kommandeur*, Hauptmann Elstermann, the

Left: FW190 being camouflaged to prevent detection by Allied reconnaissance aircraft.
Bundesarchiv

Below left: The hard-fought battle at mid-day on 25 August 1944 was between II./JG 6 and the US 367th Fighter Group. The American Group's three squadrons, the 392nd, 393rd and 394th Squadrons, flew the P-38 Lightning. The 394th Squadron's 12 Lightnings had been attacking the airfield at Clastres when II./JG 6 engaged it. The 21 Lightnings of the other two Squadrons, answering the call for help from the 394th, abandoned their attacks on airfields in the area and went to their comrades' assistance. During the battle that followed the American pilots claimed 20 FW190s destroyed; in fact II./JG 6 lost 16 aircraft, though in view of the briskness of the combat such a discrepancy is to be expected. The American force lost seven Lightnings, six of them from the 394th Squadron. Depicted is Captain Lawrence E. Blumer who led the 393rd Squadron during the action and was credited with five FW190s destroyed during it./*USAF*

forty-odd FW190s took off shortly after noon; so sketchy had our training been that this was, in fact, the first occasion on which II./JG 6 had ever flown together as a *Gruppe*. My *Staffel*, the 7th, was to fly as top-cover and so took off first; we orbitted the field while the others got airborne, then the large formation climbed away to the west with our *Staffel* about 6,000ft above the other two.

Soon after leaving the vicinity of Herpy we received new orders from the ground: enemy fighter-bombers were attacking the airfield at Chastres near St Quentin. We were to engage them. Elstermann turned the *Gruppe* on to a northerly heading and shortly afterwards I caught sight of some aircraft a few miles away to the north, below the level of our *Staffel* but above the main part of our formation. I called the *Gruppenkommandeur*: "*Achtung, Fragezeichen von rechts*" (attention, question marks – unidentified aircraft – to the right). He acknowledged my call and identified the aircraft as American P-38 Lightnings. With the sun on our backs we went after them and as we got closer I counted about twelve. Elstermann gave the order "*Zusatzbehaelter weg!*" and as the drop tanks tumbled away from the aircraft my *Staffelkapitän*, Oberleutnant Paffrath, took us down to attack. I took my *Schwarm* to follow him in a tight turn, but suddenly my Focke Wulf gave a shudder, the wing dropped and I found myself spinning helplessly into the melee below. I had to take the standard spin recovery action, pushing the stick forwards and applying opposite rudder, with the dogfight going on all around me. It was utter chaos, with Focke Wulfs chasing Lightnings chasing Focke Wulfs. I recovered from my spin and fired a burst at one Lightning, only to have to break away when another Lightning curved round and opened fire at me. Then I discovered what had caused me to spin in the first place: my drop tank was still in position and resisted all my efforts to get it to release. Since it was almost full of fuel the tank weighed about 500lbs; no wonder I could not turn as tightly as the aircraft which had got rid of their tanks!

Our initial attack hit the Americans hard and I saw some Lightnings go down. We might have been new to the business of dogfighting, but with the advantage of the sun and numbers we held the initiative. The surviving American fighters twisted and turned, trying to avoid our repeated attacks.

Then, suddenly, there seemed to be Lightnings diving on us from all directions: now it was our turn to become the hunted. Obviously far more experienced than we were in fighter-versus-fighter combat, the American pilots who had just arrived on the scene cruised overhead selecting their victims, then dived down in pairs to pick them off before zooming back to altitude. We were being chopped up by experts and I watched Focke Wulf after Focke Wulf go down.

I climbed and tried to re-join the fight, moving in to cover the tail of a Focke Wulf without any protection. But as I got there a pair of Lightnings came down after us; he went into a tight turn and as I tried to follow him I found myself spinning out of control again. I repeated this unnerving experience a couple more times before deciding to give up; my meagre experience in handling the FW190 was insufficient for this situation and the middle of a dogfight was no place to learn. I was doing nothing to help my comrades and if I stayed around much longer I would almost certainly make an easy victim for one of the Lightnings. I broke away and dived down to low altitude, making good my escape. I landed back at Herpy, taxied to my dispersal point, shut down the engine and clambered out; my flying suit was wringing wet with sweat.

Then in dribs and drabs the survivors of the fight came in, some of them bearing the scars of battle. As the afternoon wore on the magnitude of the disaster which had befallen our *Gruppe* became clear: sixteen of our aircraft had been destroyed, with fourteen pilots killed or missing and three more wounded. Amongst the missing was the *Kapitän* of the 8th *Staffel*, Leutnant Rudi Dassow, who had been one of the most successful twin-engined fighter pilots in the *Luftwaffe* with 22 kills including twelve of four-engined bombers. Our own *Staffelkapitän*, Oberleutnant Paffrath, was amongst the wounded.

The scale of the losses during the battle on 25 August came as a great shock: with so many aircraft destroyed and damaged, our fighting strength had been reduced by about a half during a single engagement. We were indeed learning the lessons of combat the hard way. Yet we had little time to mourn our comrades: the battle was continuing and the retreating German ground troops were taking a terrible beating from the Allied aircraft.

On the following day, 26 August, the surviving Focke Wulfs of II./JG6 were ordered off again, to cover the Seine crossings. Again I led my *Schwarm* and we made for our briefed patrol area near Rouen. Soon after our arrival in the battle area, however, we were 'bounced' from out of the sun by Mustangs. I never even saw the aircraft that hit me. All I heard was a loud bang and the next thing I knew my aircraft was tumbling out of the sky with part of the tail shot away. I blew off the canopy and struggled to get clear of the spinning aircraft, but my right foot became wedged under the instrument panel. After what seemed an age I managed to wrench it away, though I left my flying boot behind and my foot collided with the tailplane as I was falling clear. My parachute opened normally and I landed on the west bank of the Seine near Duclair. A reargard unit of the SS picked me up and took me to their field dressing station, where one of their doctors removed a metal splinter from my left foot and bound it up. During the night I was taken across the river on board an army ferry.

After a journey lasting over a day, in which we covered about 140 miles, they dropped me off at a Luftwaffe airfield: Juvincourt. The units spearheading the enemy advance were getting close and everyone was getting ready to pull out. Every serviceable aircraft had already left and army engineers had placed demolition charges ready to blow up the runway and taxi tracks. Somebody suggested that I might like to fly out a partially serviceable FW190, which would otherwise have to be blown up. I jumped at the chance: I thought that no flight in an aircraft could possibly be worse than the journey I had just made by road.

There were a few small problems, however: the stores at Juvincourt had either been moved out or else destroyed and they could provide me with no flying helmet, parachute or maps. There was no ammunition for the Focke Wulf's guns and the fuel tanks held sufficient petrol for only about three-quarters of an hour's flying. An old blanket was folded up and placed in the well of the seat normally occupied by the parachute, and with my foot still bandaged I was lifted into the cockpit. Just as I was about to start the engine, however, an engineering officer appeared and said that the aircraft was unfit to fly and he would accept no responsibility for it in its present condition: quite apart from several uncleared faults, it had recently been involved in a very heavy landing which had strained the tail and possibly the undercarriage as well. I told him that under the circumstances I was happy to accept responsibility for the aircraft. Freed of the possibility of future recriminations, he agreed to let me take it.

I started the engine and took off, aiming to get to Florennes near Namur in Belgium which was about 80 miles away as the crow flies. Flying without a map, however, I could not take the most direct route: I decided to follow the line of the Aisne River and canal to Sedan, then the Meuse River which flowed close to Florennes. Soon after take-off the first problem manifested itself: the undercarriage refused to retract. With the gear down the limiting speed of the FW190 was 160mph; if I was spotted by enemy fighters, I would be easy meat. Even so, I reasoned, I was far better off in an aircraft going at 160mph than a car moving at 30mph; there could be no thought to returning to Juvincourt, having got this far. I kept low to avoid trouble.

After about twenty minutes' flying, however, things began to go really wrong. I suddenly noticed that the needle of the oil temperature gauge was rising past the danger mark. This was bad news: the rear cylinders of the BMW801 always ran hot and if there was any failure in their lubrication the engine was liable to seize. Now I really was in a fix. I had no parachute so I could not bale out, and if I crash landed with the undercarriage extended and the ground was not hard enough the aircraft was liable to nose over on to its back. As the oil temperature rose still higher it became clear that I had better choose a field soon, and get the Focke Wulf down while the motor still had some life in it. If the engine failed suddenly, I should have no choice where I landed.

I picked out a reasonably large flat field and made for it. I decided to bring the Focke Wulf down in a hard side-slip to port. In that way, with a bit of luck, the undercarriage might be wiped off and the aircraft would then come to rest on its belly. It seemed a good idea, but it did not quite work out. The undercarriage proved stronger than I had expected. It held. The port wing took the main force of the impact and buckled. The aircraft then swung round, the motor struck the ground so violently that it broke right away, the fuselage then rolled over and finally came to rest upside-down. Bruised all over and covered in blood, I managed to fight my way out of the cockpit. As I stood up beside the wrecked Focke Wulf I saw men running towards me. My first horrified thought was 'Oh God, partisans!' If they caught me like this they would probably slit my throat from ear to ear. Fortunately for me, however, they turned out to be simple farmers. They took pity on my miserable condition and helped me to their village, where a German army vehicle later picked me up.

I spent the next six weeks in hospital recovering from my various wounds, then rejoined II./JG6 at Eudenbach near Bonn. When I arrived there, there were only three or four survivors out of the forty or so half-trained pilots that had set out with me to go to France in August; the remainder were either dead, wounded or in enemy prison camps. Shortly afterwards I was sent to a training unit, to help convert ex-bomber pilots on to the FW190.

My combat career as a single-engined fighter pilot had lasted exactly two missions: during the first I had a hard fight merely to stay alive, during the second I was shot down and wounded. So far as I am aware, during neither of these did my presence cause the enemy the slightest inconvenience. In the summer of 1944, the skies over France were no place for a beginner.

Left, below and right. Focke Wulf 190 spy planes. Aircraft of a reconnaissance unit, believed to be the 5. Staffel of Fernaufklaerungsgruppe 123 at Le Luc near Toulon in France in the summer of 1944. The fairing over the camera port, which identifies the aircraft as the A4/U4 photographic reconnaissance version, is just visible under the fuselage under the marking./*Bundesarchiv*

Below centre: Camera control unit, situated beneath the centre of the pilot's instrument panel. The rotatable knob enabled the pilot to adjust the framing rate of the cameras, to ensure that there was the correct overlap between adjacent pictures whatever the altitude or speed of the aircraft. The counter in the bottom left hand corner gave the amount of film remaining. *VFW-Fokker*

Below right: A split-pair of RB12.5 cameras, mounted in the rear fuselage of an FW190. These cameras were used for low altitude reconnaissance. For high Altitude work, longer focal length cameras were necessary./*VFW-Fokker*

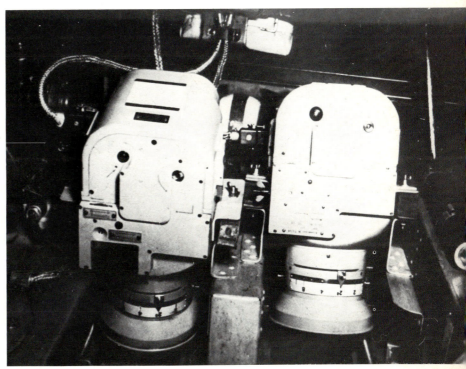

If Necessary, by Ramming
Walther Hagenah

'If your bayonet breaks, strike with the stock; if the stock gives way, hit with your fists; if your fists are hurt, bite with your teeth.'

General Mikhail Dragomirov, 'Notes for Soldiers', 1890

During the spring of 1944 the fighter units defending the German homeland faced an uncomfortable dilemma: if their aircraft were to engage the American four-engined bombers with any great chance of success, they had to carry batteries of heavy cannon or rockets; but if they were weighed down with such weapons, the defending fighters fell as easy prey to the American escorts which now ranged over the length and breadth of the country. As a solution to this problem, during the early summer two distinct types of fighter *Gruppe* emerged: *Sturmgruppen*, equipped with heavily armed and armoured versions of the FW190 flown by pilots dedicated to destroy the bombers; and *Begleitgruppen*, units equipped with comparatively lightly-armed fighters which were to hold off the escorts so that the *Sturmgruppen* could attack without interference. Walther Hagenah served with one of the *Sturmgruppen* and he explains what it meant to be a member of such a unit.

I finished my training as a fighter pilot in 1942 and immediately afterwards began operations with the First Gruppe of Jagdgeschwader 3, flying Messerschmitt 109s on the Russian front. I remained in the east for the next nine months until late in 1943, when my *Gruppe* was pulled back to Germany. Now flying the Messerschmitt 109G, we were to take part in home defence operations against the American heavy bombers.

During our initial home defence operations we experimented with several different forms of attack against the four-engined bombers: from directly behind, diving from above, diving from above and pulling up to attack from underneath, even from directly in front. Between December 1943 and May 1944 my personal score amounted to five heavy bombers, four B-17s and one B-24. But although my own and the other air defence *Gruppen* were having some success, it was clear

that far more of the heavy bombers would have to be knocked down if the Americans were to cease their devastating attacks on our homeland. Moreover, with the appearance of their long range escort fighters deep over Germany, things were getting more difficult with each month that passed.

In July 1944, when I held the rank of Leutnant, I accepted an invitation to join IV. (Sturm) Gruppe of JG3 under Hauptmann Wilhelm Moritz based at Illesheim. This was the first of several *Sturmgruppen* being formed, with the object of inflicting really heavy losses on the American bomber formations in spite of the escorts.

The *Sturmgruppe* differed in three fundamental respects from the normal fighter unit: in the men who served in it, in the aircraft that it operated and in the tactics that it used.

Pilots volunteering to join a *Sturmgruppe* had all to sign the following affidavit:

'I, . . . do solemnly undertake that on each occasion on which I make contact with an enemy four-engined bomber I shall press home my attack to the shortest range and will, if my firing pass is not successful, destroy the enemy aircraft by ramming.'

It was made clear to us that, having signed the affidavit, failure to carry out its conditions would render us liable to trial by court martial on a charge of cowardice in the face of the enemy. No man was forced to sign, however, and there were no recriminations against those who did not wish to do so; they simply did not join the ranks of the *Sturmgruppen*.

The second point of difference between a *Sturmgruppe* and a normal fighter unit was that we operated versions of the Focke Wulf 190A-8 fitted with more armour and a much heavier armament than was usual. For example the A8 R8, which I flew, carried nearly twice as much armour as the basic FW190A-8. The armour round the nose ring was thicker, as was that behind my head; in addition there was extra armour around the base of my windscreen, round the ammunition boxes of the cannon in the outer wing, and down the sides of the cockpit. Two large pieces of thick toughened glass were fitted to the canopy, one on each side, and the side pieces of the windscreen were similarly strengthened. Like the normal A-8 the aircraft carried a pair of 13mm machine guns above the engine and two 20mm cannon in the wing roots. But in the outer wings were two powerful 30mm MK108 cannon. The resultant aircraft, nicknamed the *Sturmbock*, was about 400lbs heavier than the basic FW190A-8. The extra weight meant it was a little slower in the climb rather less crisp on the controls than a normal aircraft.

With their harder breed of fighter pilot and the special aircraft, the *Sturmgruppen* were to employ tactics quite different from those previously used by fighter units. In the past we had flown in open tactical formations, attacked the bombers in twos and fours, and it was up to individual *Rotte* and *Schwarm* leaders to decide when to open fire and when to break away. In the *Sturmgruppe*, however,

Below: Leutnant Walther Hagenah, whose account appears left, flew the heavily armoured *Sturmbock* version of the FW190A-8 during the summer of 1944./*Hagenah*

it was quite different. We flew in a close arrow-head formation by *Staffeln*, with the *Staffel* leader in the front and the other aircraft in echelon on either side of him with two or three yards between each aircraft. Succeeding *Staffeln* followed close behind, each slightly lower than the one in front. When the *Sturmgruppe* leader had positioned his force behind a '*Pulk*' of bombers he would allocate his aircraft to engage different parts of the enemy formation. For example the leading *Staffel* might receive orders to engage the high squadron of bombers, the next might take on the middle squadron and the third *Staffel* might take on the low squadron of bombers. The form of the attack was therefore much more formal than anything I had used before.

Once a *Sturmstaffel* was in position about 1,000 yards behind 'its' squadron of bombers, the *Staffel* leader would order his aircraft into line abreast and, still in close formation, they would advance on the bombers. At this stage our tactics were governed by the performance of our wing-mounted 30mm cannon. Although the hexogen high explosive ammunition fired by this weapon was devastatingly effective, the gun's relatively low muzzle velocity meant that its accuracy fell off rapidly with range. And since we carried only 55 rounds per gun, sufficient for about five seconds' firing, we could not afford to waste ammunition in wild shooting from long range. To be sure of bringing down a bomber it was essential that we held our fire until we were right up close against the bombers. We were to advance like Frederick the Great's infantrymen, holding our fire until we could see 'the whites of the enemy's eyes'.

During the advance each man picked a bomber and closed on it. As our formation moved forwards the American bombers would, of course, let fly at us with everything they had. I can remember the sky being almost alive with tracer. With strict orders to withhold our fire until the leader gave the order, we could only grit our teeth and press on ahead. In fact, however, with the extra armour, surprisingly few of our aircraft were knocked down by the bombers' return fire; like the armoured knights of the Middle Ages, we were well protected. A *Staffel* might lose one or two aircraft during the advance, but the rest continued relentlessly on. In my *Gruppe* we positioned ourselves about 100 yards behind the bombers before opening fire. Then our chance came and we made the most of it. From such a range we could hardly miss and as the 30mm explosive rounds struck home we could see the structure of the enemy bombers literally falling apart in front of us. On the average three hits with 30mm ammunition would be sufficient to knock down a four-engined bomber, and the shortest burst was usually sufficient to achieve that. On four occasions during *Sturmgruppe* actions in the summer of 1944 I got into position behind an American bomber, and on each of these I shot one down: a B-24 on 7 July, B-17s on the 18th and 20th, and a further B-24 on 3 August.

So, if a *Sturmgruppe* reached a position behind a bomber 'Pulk', it could do great execution. Getting there was not as easy as it may sound, however. Sometimes our ground control was not so good as it might have been. Also, although I as a *Staffel* leader had had training in blind flying, the majority of German fighter pilots were not adequately trained in this respect and as a result even a little cloud could play havoc with our for-

mation. The greatest problem of all, however, was the American escort fighters. Flying in our special FW190s, in close formations which were quite unsuitable for fighter-versus-fighter combat, we were extremely vulnerable to attack. To enable us to get through to the bombers, therefore, we had our own escort of two normal fighter *Gruppen*; my *Sturmgruppe* had the First and Second Gruppen of Jagdgeschwader 300, equipped with Messerschmitt 109Gs, allocated for this purpose. The formation comprising the *Sturmgruppe* with its two escorting *Gruppen* was known as the *Gefechtsverband* (battle formation) and numbered about 90 aircraft. Generally our escorts were able to ward off the American fighters. But on occasions when we did come under fighter attack, our position was a difficult one: not only were our aircraft heavy but few of the *Sturmgruppe* pilots had much experience in dogfighting. So, in general, we tried to hold our close formation and press on towards the bombers even if a few enemy

Left: Close up of the cockpit of a *Sturmbock*, officially designated the FW190A-8/R8. Note the canopy side-panels of laminated glass, and also the steel armour on the side of the pilot's position mounted on the outside of the fuselage.

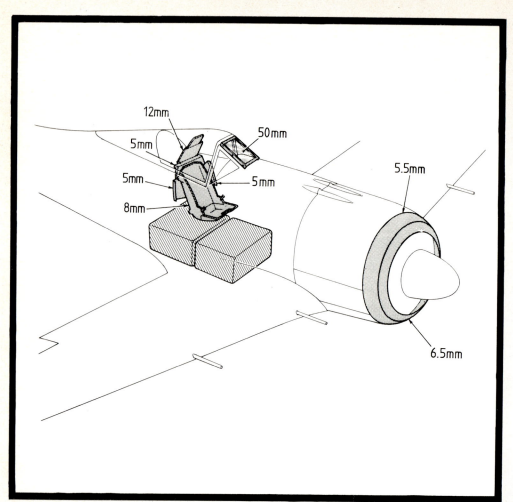

Left: Armour fitted to the standard FW190A-8. The main protection for the pilot and engine came from steel plates 5mm to 12mm thick, with a 50mm slab of bullet-resistant glass protecting the pilot's head from fire from ahead. The self-sealing fuel tanks under the pilot's seat provided him with useful protection from fire from below.

Right: Armour fitted to the FW190A-8/R8 Sturmbock, in addition to that normally carried by the A-8. The upper side panels of the cockpit were of 30mm bullet-resistant glass, the lower panels of 5mm steel plate. Steel plates protected the boxes for the 30mm high explosive cannon shells.

Below: Sturmbock aircraft of IV./JG 3, with Moritz in the lead, about to take off from Schongau in the summer of 1944./Bundesarchiv

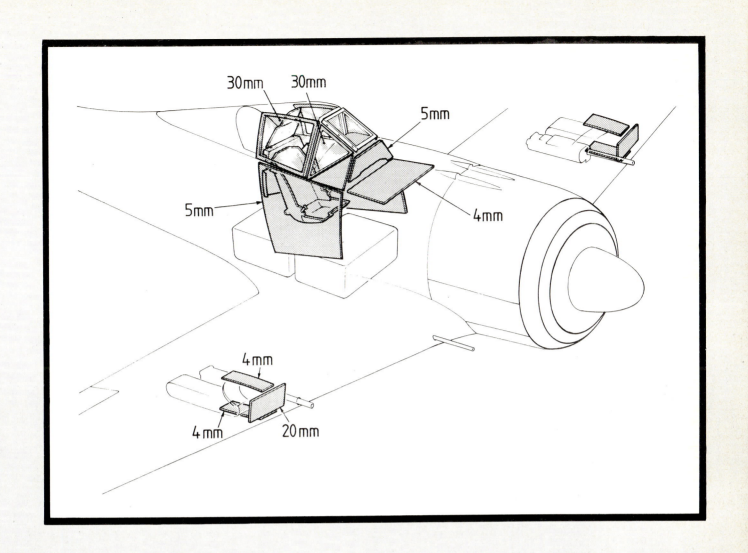

30mm 30mm 5mm 5mm 4mm 4mm 20mm 4mm

Above: Sturmgruppe pilots belonging to Hagenah's Staffel 10./JG 3, pictured in August 1944. From left to right: unidentified, Uffz Kroeber, Uffz Volz, Oberleutnant Hans Weik (Hagenah's predecessor in command of the *Staffel*, with his arm in plaster after being wounded in action), Leutnant Hagenah, Fw Schaefer, Uffz Vohl, Uffz Dreddla, Uffz Hentrich and Hfw Maxeiner (Hauptfeldwebel – the unit's senior groundcrew man). The photograph was taken at Burggen, a few miles away from the airfield at Schongau, where the men were billeted./*Hagenah*

Right: Feldwebel Hans Schaefer, wearing his leather flying jacket with the 'Whites of the Eyes' insignia worn by some *Sturmgruppe* pilots. Schaefer was credited with 27 victories, eight of them against four-engined bombers./*Schaefer*

fighters had managed to break through our escort to attack us. We thought it better to lose some aircraft and have a chance to shoot down the bombers, rather than split our formation and lose a few less aircraft but shoot down no bombers at all. But it was a difficult decision to make and on occasions it led to our taking heavy losses. On some occasions the rear *Staffel* of the *Sturmgruppe* was ordered to turn round and engage the enemy fighters that had broken through the escort, but this was the exception rather than the rule. The worst time for the enemy fighters to hit us was when the *Gefechtsverband* was forming up: if they caught us then they could throw the whole thing into confusion and the operation had to be abandoned.

During the *Sturmgruppe* operations there were, in fact, very few rammings. I did not make one and I never saw anyone else do it. The paper we had signed indicated an absolute moral commitment to bring down enemy four-engined bombers, if necessary by ram-

ming. But if we held our formation, ran the gauntlet of the bombers' defensive fire and reached a firing position 100 yards behind a bomber, with our powerful cannon it was a relatively simple matter to get a kill. There were a few occasions when people reached a firing position and found, for example, that their weapons had jammed. Then they opened their throttles, pulled up a little, dived down and rammed. By and large, however, our weapons were very reliable and that was rarely necessary.

We received no detailed instructions from our High Command on how best to ram the enemy bombers though the matter was, of course, the subject of several discussions in our crewroom. Of the pilots who made ramming attacks, about a half escaped without serious injury. One who did not was Obergefreiter Heinz Papenburg of another Sturmgruppe, II./JG4, who rammed and destroyed a B-24 on 27 August 1944. He struck the bomber going really fast and severed one of his

Below: The *Breitkeil* (wide-wedge) close formation employed by a *Sturm Staffel* moving in to attack a bomber formation; the formation is drawn to scale.

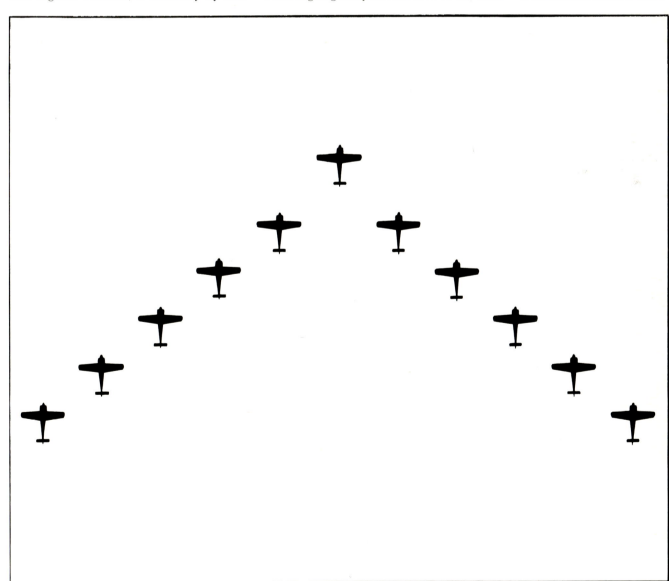

wings in the process. As he baled out of his tumbling Focke Wulf he hit the tailplane and smashed both of his legs. He descended by parachute and had to take the shock of the landing on his broken legs, which must have been terrible for him.

In September 1944 I left the *Sturmgruppe* to attend a *Verbandsfuehrerlehrgang*, a fighter leaders' course. From there I went to Erfurt, to convert ex-bomber pilots on to the FW190 for fighter operations, then to Lüben to train new *Sturmgruppe* pilots. Finally, early in 1945, I was sent to Jagdgeschwader 7 to fly the new Messerschmitt 262 jet fighter. But that is another story.

Thinking about it all now, sitting in the comfort of an armchair after more than thirty years of peace, it is easy to overemphasize the personal danger of being a *Sturmgruppe* pilot. But it should be remembered that we were in the front line in wartime, where conditions of absolute safety did not exist. Certainly the risks to us were no greater than, say, those accepted by an infantryman charging an enemy position.

As members of a *Sturmgruppe* we knew that we were a tough unit, something special, and morale was high. There were no shirkers; people like that simply did not accept the harsh conditions of membership. They enemy was systematically destroying our homeland and we were determined to hit back hard. I am proud to have been numbered amongst the *Sturmgruppe* pilots. If the conditions were ever repeated, I would do the same thing again.

Above: The Rheinmetall-Borsig MK108 30mm cannon, seen with one of its high explosive shells. The low muzzle velocity of this weapon dictated the short range engagement tactics employed by the *Sturmgruppen*; the cannon fired rounds weighing 330gr (11½oz) with a muzzle velocity of 540m/sec (1,750ft per sec) at a rate of 660 per minute.

Left: This B-17 Fortress of the 457th Bomb Group was lucky to get home to its base in eastern England, after being shot up by German fighters. The damage to the port wing is consistent with hits from one or two 30mm explosive rounds; on the average, three such hits were sufficient to bring down a heavy bomber./*USAF*

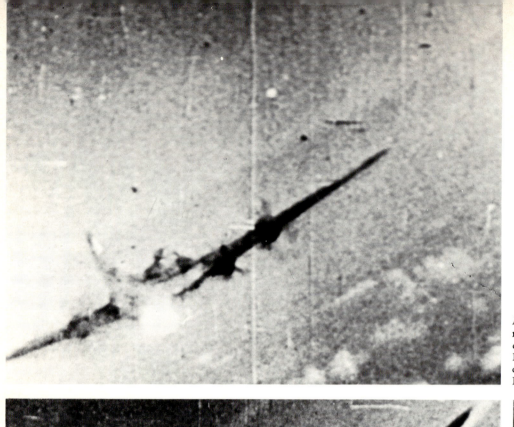

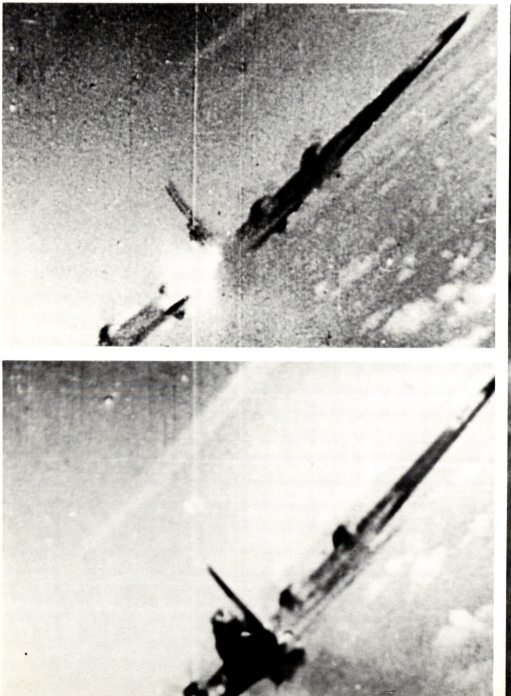

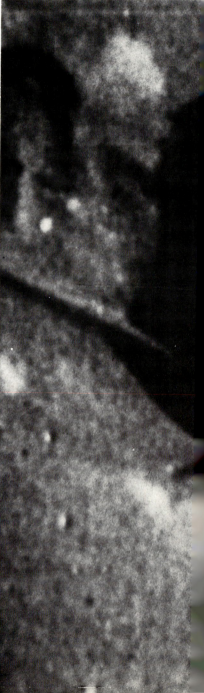

Left, below: One B-17 that did **not** get home: stills from the cine film taken by Uffz Maximowitz, when he shot down a bomber of the 447th Bomb Group on 29 April 1944.

Left: Unteroffizier Maximowitz, pictured in an FW190A-8/R8 of IV./JG 3. The muzzles of the 30mm cannon are just outboard of the undercarriage legs. This particular aircraft was not fitted with bullet-resistant glass panels on the sides of the sliding canopy./*Bundesarchiv*

The Luck of the Game
Ernst Schroeder

Like Walther Hagenah, Ernst Schroeder was a *Sturmgruppe* pilot and while serving with the Second (Sturm) Gruppe of JG300 he accounted for seven enemy aircraft of which two were heavy bombers. In this account he conveys a vividly detailed picture of one operation by his unit, that on 17 December 1944. The reader will notice some differences in tactics, compared with those described in the previous account. This is because control over minor tactical points was the prerogative of the *Gruppe* commander; also, during the course of 1944, *Strumgruppe* methods underwent some changes.

Löbnitz bei Bitterfeld, 1000 hours, 17 December 1944. It is about an hour since the four *Staffeln* of II. (Sturm) Gruppe of Jagdgeschwader 300 have been brought to readiness. The aircraft have been moved from their dispersal pens in the nearby wood, on to the airfield. On arrival the ground crews check the security of each aircraft's 72-gallon drop tank, in case the journey over the rough taxi-track has shaken it loose. Then a refuelling bowser runs down the lines of aircraft, topping up each one in turn. The thirty-odd FW190 *Sturm* aircraft, those ready for action, have been lined up on the airfield by *Schwärme*. The pilots, wearing their leather flying suits and yellow life jackets, stand around chatting close to their machines.

While all of this is going on I, an *Unteroffizier* and *Schwarm* leader, wait almost alone at the 5th Staffel dispersal area. My aircraft has developed a fault and although the ground crew are working feverishly on it, it is not yet airworthy. I hang around them impatiently: any minute now we might get the order to scramble.

Suddenly there is a bang and a red signal flare rises from the operations building: cock-

Left: An FW190A-8 of II. Sturm/JG 300 coming in to land at Loebnitz, towards the end of 1944./*Schroeder*

Far left: Unteroffizier Ernst Schroeder flew with 5./JG 300. He used this aircraft, Red 19 Works No 172733, on most of his operations between August and the end of November 1944. On 27 November the machine was hit during a fight with Mustangs, and wrecked during the subsequent belly landing at Koethen./*Schroeder*

pit readiness! My comrades climb into their aircraft and strap in, assisted by their mechanics. The stillness returns. The sun shines through the trees at the dispersal pens, now empty except for my aircraft with its panels removed and four or five 'grease monkeys' poking round inside.

Suddenly the loudspeakers round the airfield boom out: 'Achtung, Achtung, Unteroffizier Schroeder to the Gruppe Stab dispersal area, aircraft "Blue 13" is ready!' I grab my parachute and gallop the couple of hundred yards to where the aircraft stands. The Focke Wulf, a blue number '13' painted on its side, used to belong to Oberstleutnant Dahl who was our previous Geschwader commander.

Just as I am about to get into the aircraft a green flare soars into the sky: scramble! The stillness round the airfield is shattered as BMW801 engines burst into life and aircraft begin moving towards the take-off point. Hastily I buckle on my parachute and clamber into the cockpit as the mechanics help me to strap in. Damn! The position of the armoured seat and the rudder pedals has been adjusted to suit Oberstleutnant Dahl, a man who is somewhat shorter than I am. I now find myself cooped up uncomfortably with my knees bent back almost double. And there is no time to do anything about it: already the three 'young hares' of my Schwarm are moving up to the take-off point. With a roar my motor

starts (it has already been warmed up). I taxi out of the dispersal and on to the airfield, just as the last of the other aircraft are getting airborne. I line myself up on the runway and slam open the throttle; thrust along by 1,800 horse power, the machine accelerates rapidly after the others.

The formation leader on this occasion, Leutnant Bretschneider who commands the 5th Staffel, climbs away making a wide sweep to the left so that everyone can form up as rapidly as possible. I straggle along behind, gaining slowly in spite of the fact that I have cut the corner. The formation is at about 5,000 feet before I catch up with the rear end of it. Then I have to pick my way through the 'crowd', searching for my leaderless Schwarm. Fortunately I find the other three quite quickly and am in position by the time we reach Wittenberg on the Elbe; this is the assembly point for the whole Geschwader and is marked for us by a series of coloured smoke puffs from signal rounds fired by the flak people on the ground. From the right and below other fighters approach: the Messerschmitt 109s of our escorting Gruppen. After a couple of orbits at 8,000 feet the Geschwader formation is complete: some thirty FW190s of the Sturmgruppe escorted by fifty or sixty Messerschmitts. Flying just underneath the base of the clouds, we receive orders from the Fighter Divisional headquarters at Doeberitz near Berlin to climb out on a south-easterly

Right: Leutnant Klaus Bretschneider, the *Staffelkapitän* of 5./JG 300, led the *Sturmgruppe* during the action on 17 December 1944. Bretschneider led a remarkable career, starting off as a *Wilde Sau* night fighter pilot in which role he accounted for fourteen bombers. He then transfered to *Strumgruppe* operations and destroyed several bombers including one by ramming on 10 October 1944. A week after the action described, on Christmas Eve 1944, he was killed during a fight with Mustangs./*Schroeder*

Right centre: Unteroffizier Matthaus Erhardt, Bretschneider's wing man. He was seriously wounded in action on 14 January 1945./*Schroeder*

Far right: A B-24 Liberator being engaged from short range during a *Sturmgruppe* action./*IWM*

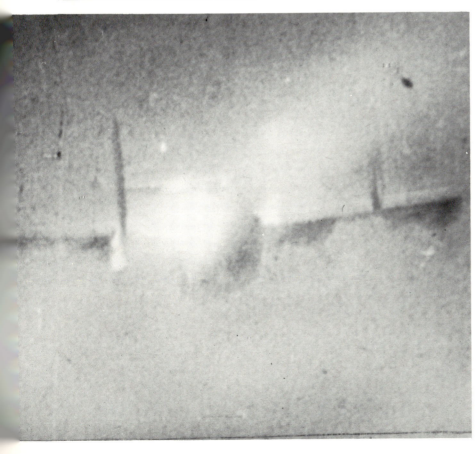

course. Over the radio they give us details of the whereabouts of the American bomber formations, which have come up from Italy and are now passing over southern Austria heading northwards.

Picking its way between the towering pillars of clouds, the formation climbs higher and higher. As we pass 13,000ft, each man clamps on his oxygen mask. In spite of Bretschneider's skilful leadership in steering the formation between the larger clouds, he is unable to prevent our passing through the occasional small one; flying in such close proximity to so many other aircraft, it is an unpleasant experience.

Once we are above cloud I have at last a little time to look round the aircraft I am flying. It is the most heavily armed Focke Wulf on our unit with two 30mm cannon, two 20mm cannon and two 13mm machine guns. Most of the aircraft in our *Gruppe* lacked the 13mm guns, while a few carried a second pair of 20mm guns in place of the wing 30mm weapons. With all of those weapons plus the additional armour, it is a typical *Sturmbock*: an unwieldy 'dungheap' weighing more than 5 tons and quite unsuitable for dogfighting. That and the cramped sitting position will make it difficult to carry out the task assigned to me for this operation: with my *Schwarm* I am to provide the *Sturmgruppe* with a final line of protection from attacks by enemy escort fighters. My usual aircraft, now sitting uselessly on the ground, is a normal FW190A-8 without extra guns or armour.

The formation continues its climb into the clear blue winter sky, with a few course corrections from the ground. From time to time, at around 18,000 feet, short condensation trails form behind our aircraft but they disappear almost immediately. For some time the radio has been silent; perhaps we are off on another *Gammeleinsatz* (wild goose chase). Our feelings are mixed, alternating between fear and hope.

We begin to receive further reports from the ground: the incoming bomber formation is on a northerly heading *Hanni 80* (altitude of enemy aircraft 8,000 metres, 26,000 feet). Far beneath us the Silesian landscape unrolls. Beyond our formation there is nothing else to be seen in the sky: no other condensation trails, no glittering reflections from other aircraft. It is all deceptively peaceful.

Within a few seconds, the picture changes completely. A series of crackling orders and course changes come through our earphones, each one more urgent and impatient than the last. Finally the controller announces: 'You have the *dicke Autos* (heavy bombers) ahead! You should be able to see them now!' We all stare into the sky: nothing.

One thing is clear, however: this is going to

Ground running an
FW190A-8/R8 at Loebnitz. The
man walking beside the port
wing tip is Leutnant Spenst,
the *Staffelkapitän* of 8./JG 300.
Schroeder

be no *Gammeleinsatz*. In each aircraft the pilot checks that his gunsight is switched on and his armament safety switches are to 'fire'. Suddenly we hear Bretschneider's urgent call on the radio: '*Victor, Victor von Specht Anton. Ich sehe dicke Autos! Wir machen Pauke-Pauke!*' (loose translation: 'Roger, Roger this is Woodpecker leader. I see the bandits! Tally-Ho!) With my four aircraft I have to protect the *Gruppe* from enemy fighters coming in from the left, so I position my *Schwarm* about 300 feet above the main body of the formation to get a better overall view. Then I catch sight of the glittering reflections of the sun on the uncamouflaged American bombers: they are obliquely to the left of us and at the same altitude, about 25,000 feet. Still a long way away, the stately enemy formation crosses in front of us from left to right. I carefully search the sky for enemy escorts, but I can make out only three or four condensation trails above the bombers.

On the order, each FW190 lets go of its drop tank and they tumble earthwards. Then Bretschneider swings our formation a little to the left, to put us on a reciprocal heading to the enemy bombers. The leading enemy 'combat box' passes by with a wide margin: it comprises fifteen or twenty B-24 Liberators with red-painted tails, an imposing sight. Just before the second 'combat box' comes past, our formation begins a moderately tight right-hand turn to slot into position between it and the third. With my *Schwarm* I continue a few seconds longer straight ahead, keeping a sharp look-out to the front and above for enemy fighters; still there are none. Then I curve round after the rest of our formation. The *Sturmgruppe* is now directly in front of me, about 150 feet below; I have a grandstand view of the attack as it unfolds. Behind me is the third 'combat box'; but is it too far away for the bombers' front guns to present any danger and in any case the bombers themselves are flying much slower than we are. We are now flying exactly in the stream of enemy bombers, rapidly overhauling the second 'combat box'. Above us I can make out a few P-38 fighters, but it seems that we have taken them by surprise and they do not come down to attack. Perhaps they are calling up reinforcements.

In front of me the drama unfolds rapidly. The bombers open up a furious defensive fire, filling the sky with tracer. It seems that none of us can avoid being hit. We at the rear of the formation weave a little, to make things difficult for the American gunners. The entire *Sturmgruppe* moves in at full throttle, to close the range on the enemy bombers as rapidly as possible. At 300 yards the main body of the FW190s opens up with their 20mm and 30mm cannon, the murderous trains of high explo-

sive shells streaking out towards the Liberators. Within seconds two of the giant aircraft have exploded into great fireballs, while several others have caught fire and are falling out of the formation. In strong contrast to the strict radio discipline that had reigned previously, the ether becomes a babble of voices: '*Horrido!* (I've got him) He's on fire!' 'All assemble to the right and above' 'I'm hit, baling out' and so on.

With my *Schwarm* I now close in on the shattered enemy formation. I make a quick check to see that the sky behind us is clear of enemy fighters, then I lead my Focke Wulfs in to attack. I select a Liberator and at 300 yards I press the firing button. Damn! Nothing happens! The bomber gets closer and closer, 50 – 40 – 30 yards, an ideal firing position! Swearing like a deranged man I press and re-press the electrical circuit breakers for the guns and the firing button, but still I cannot get them to fire. On either side of me my *Schwarm* comrades fire like mad and score hit after hit on their targets. At the last moment I push down the nose of my Focke Wulf, then pull up with the rest of the *Gruppe* to the right and above the bombers. Looking around, the sky is like a chaotic circus: whirling and fluttering pieces of aircraft, an entire wing falling complete with engines and propellers still turning, several parachutes, and some of our aircraft battling with the few P-38 escort fighters that have reached us.

Enraged and frustrated, I continue with my efforts to discover the reason for the failure of my armament. But all is in vain, I cannot get off a single round. Now I am no use to anyone so, infuriated with the aircraft, I push down the nose to dive away steeply and break off the action.

Earlier in the year, under the rules of membership of a *Sturmgruppe*, I should have been expected to bring down an American bomber by ramming if my guns had failed to do so. But by December 1944 the shortage of trained fighter pilots in the Luftwaffe is so grave that this suicidal form of attack is no longer required. When the facts of the matter are made known to my commander, afterwards, I shall receive no reproof.

I land my Focke Wulf at Liegnitz in Silesia at 1230 hours, having been airborne for almost exactly two hours. There my aircraft is quickly refuelled and I take off again at 1410 hours and land back at Loebnitz twenty minutes later. I taxi the machine back to the *Gruppe Stab* dispersal area where it had come from. No sooner have I shut down the engine then I begin to tear a strip off the ground crewman for giving me an aircraft whose guns do not work. One of them reaches into the cockpit, however, and quietly points to an extra gun safety switch fitted to this

particular FW190: it is still set to 'safe'. The system is slightly different from that fitted in any of our other aircraft and I could not have known about it.

Looking back on the incident today, more than thirty years later, I am pleased for the sake of the ten American airmen on board that Liberator that my guns did not work. Had they done so the bomber would almost certainly have been torn to pieces and they would have had little chance of survival.

Above left: Trial installation of the X-4 joy-stick control unit fitted into the instrument panel of an FW190 fighter.

Centre left and below: On 11 August 1944, near Gutersloh, an FW190 carried out the first airborne firing of the Rhurstahl X-4 air-to-air guided missile. Powered by a liquid fuel rocket motor, the X-4 was directed by command signals transmitted down thin wires unreeled from the weapon as it sped towards the target. With a maximum range of about 3,000 yards, the X-4 weighed 132lbs at launch. The 44lb high explosive warhead was fitted with acoustic proximity, impact and self-destroying fuses; the acoustic proximity fuse employed a microphone tuned to the noise of a heavy bomber, and set off the warhead as it passed close to the target. Had the war continued, the X-4 would almost certainly have been the first air-to-air guided missile to be used in action.

Eastern Front Jabo
Werner Gail

Werner Gail flew Focke Wulf 190 fighter-bombers on the Eastern Front, where the actions were characterised by the large ground forces involved and the vastness of the distances. In this account he describes his unit's tactics to slow up Russian armoured thrusts that had broken through the German front line – a type of mission which is of more than passing interest to current NATO planners.

In June 1944, while I was serving as a *Leutnant* flying Focke Wulf 190F fighter bombers with the Third Gruppe of Schlachtgeschwader 3, my unit was suddenly ordered to the eastern front. The massive steamroller of the Russian summer offensive had just begun its move westwards and almost immediately the enemy had broken through in several places; the enemy armoured units were thrusting ahead, right into our undefended rear areas.

As rapidly as possible we moved first to Duenaburg in Lithuania, then a little further east to Idriza in Russia. Our task was to do all we could to delay the trusts, to give the German ground forces time to improvise defensive positions to stop the rush. Wherever there was a hole in the front, it was our job to try to plug it.

During this period the ground situation was so fluid that we had to start each day with an armed reconnaissance: two or three *Schwärme* were sent to patrol different parts of the area assigned to our *Gruppe*, to see if the enemy had moved and if so where. Since we soon came to know our area well and we knew where the enemy had been the night before, we had a good idea where to start looking for him the following morning. Also, whenever enemy armoured units had broken through, they would advance through open country which made the task of finding them much easier.

Once the reconnaissance *Schwärme* had returned and their pilots reported on the latest enemy positions, the *Gruppe* was allocated its targets for the day in order of importance.

Our Focke Wulfs were armed with two 13mm machine guns and two 20mm cannon, which we used for strafing attacks. The bombs we used during these operations were mainly 550 and 1,100lbs and also SD-2, SD-4 and SD-10 bomblets carried in large numbers in containers.

When we found enemy units moving forwards unopposed, as a matter of policy we concentrated our attacks on the soft-skinned supply vehicles; these were relatively easy to

Below: FW190F ground attack aircraft, showing the armour fitted to this version *in addition* to that normally carried by the FW190A-8 fighter.

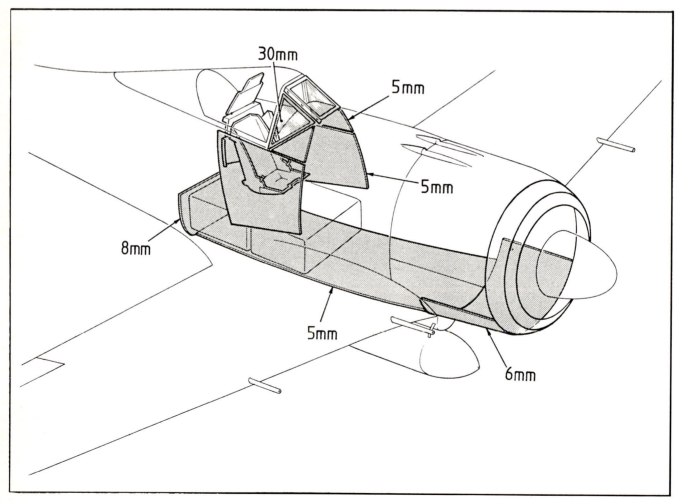

knock out with machine-gun and cannon fire and we knew that without frequent replenishments of fuel the tanks spearheading the advance would not get far. If the enemy armoured units were actually in contact with our ground forces, however, then the tanks themselves were our main target.

The normal unit during these attacks was the four-aircraft *Schwarm*, though against the larger enemy troop concentrations sometimes as many as twelve aircraft would be used. Usually we would approach our target at altitudes around 6,000ft, above the effective reach of the enemy light flak, though if there was much cloud about we would keep underneath it so as to maintain contact with the ground. Against the enemy tanks and armoured vehicles we usually make skip bombing attacks, running in at speeds of around 300mph at between 15 and 30 feet above the ground and releasing the bomb just as the tank disappeared beneath our engine cowling. The 550lb bombs used during these attacks would either skip off the ground and into the tank, or else smash straight into the tank; the bombs were fused with a one second delay, to give us time to get clear before they went off. It was a very accurate form of attack and we used it often against the tanks we caught in open country. Once we had released our bombs, we would use up our cannon and machine gun ammunition against suitable targets round about.

During the first part of the Russian offensive the pace of operations of our *Gruppe* was very high, sometimes with as many as seven or eight sorties per day. On the average the sorties lasted only about half an hour; the enemy was never very far away. Sometimes we caught Russian units that had outrun their flak cover and then we could do a lot of damage and suffer hardly any losses ourselves. But if the enemy units did have proper flak cover our losses were sometimes heavy. Only rarely did we come into contact with Russian fighters. I personally saw them on only two occasions and on neither did we lose an aircraft. Even so, the general view of the more experienced people on the Eastern Front was that in the summer of 1944 the Russian fighters were much more active than they had been during previous years.

Throughout July, August, September and October 1944 our ground troops were steadily pushed back further and further. Army Group North, with which our *Gruppe* was operating, was squeezed up into the Courland Peninsula in Latvia and the main Russian

Left: Leutnant Werner Gail, of III./SG 3, with his FW190F fighter bomber./*Gail*

FW190F fighter bombers of
Schlachtgeschwader 2,
photographed at Sopoc/Puszta
in Hungary in January 1945.
via Obert

thrust went past us heading westwards: we were cut off.

Initially, as I have said, the pace of operations was very high. But from the end of August the general fuel shortage throughout the Luftwaffe began to make itself felt and we had to reduce consumption. Towards the end, it sometimes happened that before missions our aircraft had to be towed by oxen from their dispersals to the take-off point; and after landing we had to shut down our engines immediately and await the towing crew. When the Russians were actually attacking the pocket, however, the High Command was initially able to scrape some fuel together and while the battles lasted we often flew as many as five sorties a day. Gradually even these emergency stores of fuel were exhausted and we flew less and less; during the first two months of 1945 the *Gruppe* flew hardly at all. Throughout our time in the pocket we had plenty of aircraft, plenty of pilots and plenty of bombs; but hardly any fuel.

My *Gruppe* stayed in the Courland pocket until the very end. Only on the day of the armistice, 8 May 1945, did we receive permission to fly our aircraft out. That afternoon I took off from Nikas with four ground crewmen squeezed into my Focke Wulf. For my passengers the flight of almost 600 miles to Schleswig Holstein was long and uncomfortable; but neither so long nor so uncomfortable as was the Russian captivity for those left behind.

Ferrying the Focke Wulfs
Adolf Dilg

In his earlier account Adolf Dilg described the fighter-bomber operations over the Mediterranean area, leading up to his being wounded and taken off operational flying at the end of 1943. This was not the end of his flying career, however; semi-fit pilots were sent to second-line tasks, to release fit pilots for operational units. Yet, as Dilg now recounts, even for a second-line pilot the closing months of the war were not without excitement.

Following my medical downgrading in October 1943, after my repaired right arm was found to be too weak for operational flying, I spent a short period flying communications aircraft. Then I was sent to the Arado factory at Warnemunde near Rostock, for duties as a test and delivery pilot. By the spring of 1944

the factory was turning out Focke Wulf 190s at the rate of about 180 per month. These all had to be test flown, then ferried to units all over the place: to Russia, to the north of Norway, to France and to Italy.

During the delivery flights we flew with loaded guns; with Allied long-range fighters becoming more and more active over our territory, the likelihood of having to face attack while in transit increased with each month that passed. Some of our ferry pilots were shot down but I was lucky. The only time I met enemy fighters, four Mustangs near Nuremburg, an Me262 jet fighter chanced on the scene and the American fighters broke off the chase.

During the final stages of the war, as more and more German workers were called up into

Right: Feldwebel Adolf Dilg, pictured in the cockpit of an FW190 with his dog Peter, prior to a delivery flight./*Dilg*

Below: An FW190F fighter bomber, fitted with dust filters on each side of the engine cowling, starting up in a cloud of smoke at Tutow./*Dilg*

Far right, top: Ground running an FW190F prior to a delivery flight. The '75' painted in black on the cowling was a factory marking./*Dilg*

Far right, centre: Low altitude delivery flight in an FW190. *Dilg*

Far right, bottom: Ground crew at Tutow making final adjustments to an FW190F. *Dilg*

the army, their places in the aircraft factories were taken by forced labourers and other foreign workers of doubtful reliability. Aircraft were sabotaged in all sorts of ways. Sometimes we would find bits of metal swarf in electrical junction boxes, or sand in oil systems. On two or three occasions brand new Focke Wulfs took off for their maiden flights and as they lifted off the ground one of the wheels fell off; the pin holding the wheel retaining ring had 'accidentally' come adrift. Once, when I was delivering an aircraft, the engine suddenly burst into flames. I baled out and the aircraft crashed into a marshy area where the water rapidly extinguished the flames. When the wreckage was examined, it was found that somebody had jammed a couple of pyrotechnic flares between cylinders Nos 7 and 9, the two at the bottom of the rear row which became hottest when the engine was running. During the delivery flight the cylinders had duly heated up, 'cooked-off' the flares, and up went the engine. Every time we had such an incident the Gestapo would make a lot of fuss, but although they would take the odd scapegoat the problem of sabotage was one we had to live with.

During the course of 1944 the steady contraction of the area occupied by our forces became vividly clear to those of us delivering the aircraft, as our flights became progressively shorter; by the autumn the majority of aircraft could be delivered direct, without the need for a refuelling stop en route.

When the end came, even we delivery pilots became caught up in the rush to evacuate German women and children from areas threatened by the Russian advance. In the middle of March 1945 we received orders to evacuate all aircraft from Kolberg (now Kolobrzeg in Poland), just before it fell. I flew out a Focke Wulf 190 with the armour plate behind my seat removed and in its place there crouched a twelve-year-old girl; the radio had been removed from the rear fuselage and there was huddled her mother, who had first to remove all metal objects from her clothing so as not to interfere with the master compass beside her. Another of the ferry pilots, Gefreiter Herzmann, flew an FW190 out of Kolberg with a young child on each knee and their mother in the rear fuselage. Evacuation transport: it must have been the purpose furthest from Kurt Tank's mind, when he had conceived the fighter seven years earlier.

Left: The fighter ace Hauptmann Walter Nowotny (in uniform) pictured with Focke Wulf test pilots, from left to right, Hans Kampmeier, Werner Fink, Rolf Mondry and Alfred Motsch. Nowotny was killed in action in November 1944 in an Me262 jet fighter. At the time of his death his confirmed victory total stood at 258, the great majority of these achieved while flying the FW190 with JG 54 on the Eastern Front./*Sander*

Right: Damaged aircraft outside the burning factory at Tutow, where FW190s were assembled. The plant was attacked by American heavy bombers on four occasions, on 20 February, 9 April and on 13 and 19 May 1944./*Dilg*

Below: One of the few two-seat FW190 conversion trainers built, this A8/U1 was probably photographed at the Ago works at Oschersleben. *Redemann.*

Enter the Long-nosed Dora

Oskar-Walter Romm

> If necessity is the mother of invention, warfare is the mother of development.
>
> *Sir Christopher Foxley-Norris*

In the summer of 1944 the first examples of the re-engined Focke Wulf 190 Dora began to roll off the production lines. This fighter, although like its predecessor it had the appearance of a radial-engined machine, was in fact powered by the higher-powered liquid-cooled in-line Junkers Jumo 213 engine; the annular cooling radiator was situated immediately behind the propeller. Oberleutnant Oskar-Walter Romm flew this type, the final version of the FW190 to go into action in large numbers, and he now gives his recollections.

I first saw the Dora-9 in December 1944, at Stargard near Stettin. The aircraft had just been delivered from the Focke Wulf works at Marienburg near Danzig in East Prussia. At that time I belonged to the IV. (Sturmgruppe) of Jagdgeschwader 3 'Udet', which operated the FW190A-8 and was engaged in the air defence of the Reich. In January 1945 I was appointed *Staffelkapitän* of the 15th Staffel; the following month, as the oldest *Staffelkapitän* (I was just over 25 years old) I was given command of the whole *Gruppe*. From Stargard our task was to mount bombing and strafing attacks against Russian forces advancing towards Berlin and Stettin.

I was very keen to get hold of the FW190D-9, because I could see that before long we should be engaged in a war on two fronts against, on the one side the Russians and, on the other, the British and American fighters and bombers. For such fighting I considered the D-9 to be the ideal aircraft. I succeeded in getting one full *Staffel* equipped with this

Below: Focke Wulf 190D-9s of Stab IV./JG 3, at Prenzlau in March 1945. The aircraft are at readiness, with parachutes on their tails./*Romm*

version, as well as my *Gruppe Stab* with four of these aircraft plus one reserve. To get some of the aircraft we had to rescue them from airfields about to be overrun by the enemy, in spite of the risks involved.

All of our Dora-9s were fitted with the Jumo 213A engine which, with water methanol injection, developed 2,240 horse power. As an air superiority and interceptor fighter the FW190D-9 handled better than the FW190A; it was faster and had a superior rate of climb. During dogfights at altitudes of between about 10,000 feet and 24,000 feet, usual when engaging the Russians, I found that I could pull the FW190D into a tight turn and still retain my speed advantage. In the FW190A I had flown previously, during dogfights I had often to reduce to minimum flying speed in the turn. In the descent the Dora-9 picked up speed much more rapidly than the A type; in the dive it could leave the Russian Yak-3 and Yak-9 fighters standing.

My last combat mission was on 24 April 1945, to the south of Stettin, when with my wing man I attacked a formation of Russian 'Stormovik' ground attack aircraft. I selected full emergency power and with our superior speed we went right through the Russian fighter escort without difficulty. I was just about to open fire on one of the Ilyushins when my cooling gills suddenly opened automatically and the oil and coolant temp-

Left: Oberleutnant Oskar-Walter Romm flew FW190D-9s with *IV./JG 3* during the final stages of the war. When he was invalided out of action on 24 April 1945 his victory score stood at 92./*Romm*

Below: An early production Dora-9, straight out of the factory./*VFW-Fokker*

erature gauges showed that the engine was overheating. Either my engine had been hit by enemy fire or it had suffered a failure. I broke off the action by rolling over on to my back and pulling away in a steep dive. The Russian fighters endeavouring to follow were soon left behind and abandoned the chase.

The combat had taken place over an area where the Russians had just broken through so I flew for as long as possible on my dying engine, towards the south-west and the German front line. From the exhausts a thin line of smoke trailed behind the aircraft, becoming gradually thicker and darker before thinning again with a lot of sparks. As the last of the lubricating oil burned away between the aluminium pistons and the steel cylinder block, the engine burst into flames.

By now I was over friendly territory and I wanted to bale out, but there was not enough height. The engine stopped altogether and what followed was half way between a crash and a crash landing. As a result I suffered a fractured skull, facial injuries, brain concussion as well as other less serious injuries. Later that day I was picked up by men of my unit and taken to the Luftwaffe hospital at Wismar. My part in the war was over.

Below: This dramatic photograph of a Dora-9 was taken from the attack camera of an American B-26 Marauder, after it had released its bombs on a railway target in Germany. *USAF*

Left: Romm's personnal FW190D-9, bearing the *Gruppenkommandeur* chevrons in front of the fuselage marking./*Romm*

Below: Romm's reserve FW190D-9, on the ground at Prenzlau. The aircraft bore an adjutant's chevron on the fuselage, but in fact Romm's adjutant was not qualified as a fighter pilot and never flew it. *Romm*

An Introduction to Beethoven
Bernhard Jope

Left: A fully operational *Beethoven,* an FW190 mounted on an explosive-laden Junkers 88, seen in its camouflaged blast pen at Oranienburg early in 1945. This was almost certainly one of the aircraft intended for the abortive *Eisenhammer* operation. *Schliephake*

'You will usually find that the enemy has three courses of action open to him. And of these he will adopt the fourth.

Helmut von Moltke

During the latter half of 1944 Luftwaffe staff officers completed plans for a powerful one-off attack on power stations in the Moscow and Gorky regions, on which Russian armament production depended to a large extent. The weapon chosen for their destruction was code-named *Beethoven*: a Focke Wulf 190 or Messerschmitt 109 fighter, rigidly mounted on top of a Junkers 88 bomber with the crew cabin removed and a 7,800lb warhead mounted in its place in the nose. At one time it was intended that Bernhard Jope should lead part of the attacking force; this is his story.

I began my operational career as a bomber pilot in 1941, flying the four-engined Focke Wulf Kondor against Allied shipping in the Atlantic. In 1943 I took command of Kampf-geschwader 100 which, equipped with the Dornier 217, made the first-ever attacks on shipping using air-to-surface guided missiles. Following the fuel crisis in the summer of 1944, caused by the Allied bombing attacks on the German oil industry, the German bomber force was reduced to a shadow of its former strength. My own *Geschwader* was gradually run down and, in January 1945, disbanded altogether.

At the time of the demise of KG100 I held

the rank of *Oberstleutnant* and I was sent to take command of Kampfgeschwader 30. The unit had given up its bombers and its pilots were being retrained to fly fighters; we expected to take our place with other units operating in the air defence of the Reich.

After a short course in flying the Focke Wulf 190 and the Messerschmitt 109, I moved to my *Geschwader* headquarters airfield at Ruzyne near Prague. A few days after my arrival, I received orders to make myself and my senior officers available for a top-secret briefing from officers of Goering's personal staff. The officers duly arrived and the main part of the briefing was given by a civilian professor from the intelligence department. He began by telling us about *Beethoven*, the code-name of one of the 'secret weapons' from which great things were expected. This one comprised an explosive-laden Junkers 88 bomber, on top of which was rigidly mounted a Focke Wulf 190 or a Messerschmitt 109 fighter. Controlling the combination from the cockpit of the fighter, the pilot was to take it to the target area, aim the whole thing at it, then release the lower explosive aircraft which would continue straight on and explode against the target. The lower component was fitted with a special shaped-charge warhead weighing 7,800 pounds of which 3,800 pounds was high explosive – sufficient to make a few alterations to any target it hit! His task complete, the pilot was to return home in the fighter.

Below: A training version of the *Beethoven*, with the original Ju 88 cockpit left in place and occupied by a second pilot who landed the combination at the end of the flight.

Beethoven promised several advantages over a conventional bomber. It could deliver an extremely destructive warhead to a target with reasonable accuracy; moreover, if the attack was planned so that the approach was made during the hours of darkness and the target was reached at first light, the pilot made the dangerous return flight through the alerted enemy defences in a high performance fighter with an excellent chance of avoiding interception. During the flight to the target the fighter drew its fuel from the bomber's tanks, so that at the time of separation the former's tanks were almost full.

The professor then went on to outline the operation which was in an advanced state of preparation, for which *Beethoven* was to be used. Code-named *Eisenhammer* (iron hammer), it involved a large scale co-ordinated air strike on the important power stations feeding Russian industry in the Moscow and Gorky regions. These targets, comparatively small and well-protected by concrete, were almost invulnerable to attack by ordinary bombs. If we could deliver one or two *Beethoven* warheads on each, however, it would be a different matter. If the equipment in the power stations could be destroyed or damaged, the Russians would certainly find it difficult to effect repairs; many of the turbines and much of the generating equipment had originally come from Germany, before the war.

We were then informed that our *Geschwader*, KG30, was one of those chosen to fly the *Beethoven* combinations during the *Eisenhammer* operations. So that was why all of my pilots had been re-trained to fly fighters . . . We learned that many of the combinations earmarked for the operation were ready and work on putting together the remainder was proceeding at the highest priority. The first of these aircraft would be delivered to Ruzyne shortly and training for the operation was to begin immediately. We left the two-hour briefing breathless with excitement. The enemy had been having things his own way for too long; now, at last, we could see a chance for us to strike back hard.

A few days after the briefing the first of the combinations arrived at Ruzyne. It looked such an ungainly machine, sitting at its dispersal point. This was a training version of the *Beethoven*, on which the Ju88 retained its normal crew cabin in which sat the pilot who landed the thing at the end of the flight. The explosive head was fitted only for an operational flight and when it was carried the combination could not be landed. To get into the cockpit of the fighter one had to climb up a long ladder placed against the wing. Climbing it, I felt rather like a window cleaner! The cockpit of the fighter was about 18ft high, which felt a bit odd; although when I was seated my head was in fact little higher than it was when I was in a Focke Wulf Kondor on the ground. In the FW190 there was a small extra panel underneath the main instrument panel, which carried the instruments and

Below: Major Bernhard Jope, as he then was, shaking hands with Adolf Hitler on the occasion of the presentation of the Oak Leaves to the *Ritterkreuz*, at Berchtesgarden early in April 1944. Nearest the camera stands Major Kurt Buehligen, who flew with JG 2 and ended the war credited with 112 victories, all in the West./*Jope*

Right: Rear view of a *Beethoven* combination, showing the improvised boarding arrangements for the pilot of the fighter.

Below: Seven *Beethoven* combinations of Kampfgeschwader 30, Jope's unit, photographed at Prague/ Ruzyne on 20 February 1945 soon after training began, from an Allied reconnaissance aircraft. The fighters above the Junkers 88s are hardly visible, but the shadows they threw on the ground show up clearly.

switches necessary to control the Ju88. The main flying controls were controlled by the movement of those in the fighter. There were separate controls to raise the undercarriage of the bomber after take-off (during training flights the undercarriage of the FW190 remained locked down. because the path of travel of the inwards-folding legs would have been blocked by the main supporting struts).

The big day came when I made my first flight in the *Beethoven*. Possibly because I had expected all sorts of difficulties with this unusual aircraft, and therefore handled it even more carefully than was usual with a new type, my first flight was a bit of an anti-climax. I simply started up, taxied out, took-off and tried a few turns to get the feel of the thing; it was all quite straightforward. So far as I can remember, none of my other pilots had any problems with the combination either. The initial flights were made with the lower component carrying little fuel and no warhead, so it was not very heavy and this made the combination easy to handle; during later flights the lower component was made progressively heavier.

Cruising in the *Beethoven* felt a little strange, as one was sitting in a fighter but the controls had the feel of those of a bomber. It handled like a normal Junkers 88, but there was a little more inertia during manoeuvres and so one had to be careful especially when close to the ground. During flight all three engines were kept running; on their power the combination was, perhaps surprisingly, about 30mph faster then the equivalent version of the Ju88 by itself. If there was an engine failure, the combination handled just like any other three-engined aircraft: if the centre engine failed there was no problem, because one was left with an ordinary twin-engined aircraft; if one of the bomber's engines failed, there was less of a tendency to swing than with a normal twin-engined type. Engine handling was in many ways similar to that of the old *Tante Ju*, the Junkers 52 three-engined transport. I personally never lost an engine while flying the *Beethoven*, but I anticipated no serious problems if it had occurred.

Throughout the flight, when controlled from the cockpit of the fighter, the Junkers 88's control surfaces were operated by a special type of automatic pilot. The pilot could select one of two positions: *Reiseflug* (cruising flight) or *Automatik*. The in-flight manoeuvres were made on *Reiseflug*; on this setting the movements of the stick and rudder pedals in the fighter were relayed electrically to the automatic pilot in the Ju88, which then moved its control surfaces by the corresponding amount – it was probably the world's first fly-by-wire aircraft control system to enter service. On *Automatik* the autopilot held the aircraft on whatever heading or attitude had been established; this position could be selected to ease the pilot's work load on the way to the target, and was also used when the combination was lined up for the final dive to the target immediately before the pilot fired the explosive bolts to disengage the fighter.

During our training flights in the *Beethoven* we had to keep our eyes open for Allied long-range fighters; by that stage of the war nowhere was safe from them. On one occasion Spitfires carried out a low level strafing attack on Ruzyne, shooting up some of our aircraft. Our flak defences opened up, but the British pilots demonstrated their contempt for the gunners' efforts by performing victory rolls as they climbed away. We were most impressed by this display by the sporting Royal Air Force.

When the *Geschwader*'s training programme was in the initial stages with the *Beethoven*, I received the order to hand over command to Oberst Hanns Heise. I had no experience of operations over Russia whereas he had a great deal, so he was better qualified than I was to lead the unit during *Eisenhammer*. I moved out to take up a staff appointment, but in the event I did not miss anything. The war situation deteriorated so rapidly that by the time there were sufficient aircraft and trained crews to carry out the operation against the power stations, at the end of March 1945, the necessary forward airfields had been lost to the enemy. The targets were beyond the reach of *Beethoven* and operation *Eisenhammer* had to be abandoned. Those combinations that were not destroyed on the ground, either by the enemy or by our own troops as they withdrew, were for the most part expended against the Russian crossings over the Oder River.

For my part, I have never doubted that had the necessary airfields been available, the *Beethoven* attack on the Russian power stations would have caused considerable disruption to the enemy war economy. Whether this would have had any serious effect on the course of the war is a matter for debate but one thing is certain: had that attack been mounted, it would have made a wonderful story for this book!

Below: Inside the cockpit of the FW190 half of the 'Beethoven' combination. The central panel carried the auto-pilot controls and the propeller pitch indicators and combined boost/rpm gauges for the Ju88's engines. The modified panel bears all the signs of a hastily-executed piece of work.

This FW190A-5 was one of the first to be modified specifically for night-bombing operations. As well as landing lights in the port wing, it carries flat plates above the engine exhausts to shield the pilot's eyes from the glare of the flames./VFW-Fokker

Night Jabo

'In general, I believe that night attacks are good only when one is so weak that one dare not attack the enemy in daylight.'

Frederick the Great

Even now, in the 1970s, night ground attack operations are considered to be one of the most difficult aspects of combat flying. Franz Zueger was flying such missions in a high performance fighter-bomber during the early months of 1945 and here he outlines the methods used.

From the end of my flying training in 1942 until the middle of 1944 I served as an instructor, teaching pilots to fly the Dornier 17, the Heinkel 111 and the Junkers 52. In August 1944 I left the school expecting to go to one of the units then forming with the Messerschmitt 262 jet fighter; but there was an administrative foul-up somewhere along the line and I ended up joining Schnellkampfgeschwader 107, a training unit for pilots flying Focke Wulf 190 fighter-bombers situated at Tutow near Rostock.

At Tutow the conversion course was rudimentary in the extreme. We were simply shown round the cockpit and given a set of pilots' notes. When we felt we were ready for our first flight we mentioned it to our 'instructor', who gave us an aircraft and off we went. By that time I was quite an experienced pilot and I had little trouble getting the Focke Wulf airborne. I merely held the stick central, pushed open the throttle and the next thing I knew I was airborne. Landing this lively

aircraft was, however, another matter. The first time I tried it I had to abandon the first five or six approaches. Each time, feeling I was likely to undershoot the runway, I had applied what would have been sufficient power to extend the glide of a bomber; but that was far too much for the Focke Wulf and each time it would leap away like a whipped racehorse. In the end I did learn to ease the throttle open by the required small amount and I put down the fighter safely. After a few more trips in the FW190 I begun to feel at home with it and found it a pleasant and docile machine to fly.

There followed a short period during which I made some fighter-bomber attacks against Russian troops advancing into Poland, and another in which I flew as a *Wilde Sau* night fighter over Berlin. Then in January 1945, by which time I held the rank of *Fahnenjunker Feldwebel*, I was sent to the Ergaenzungskampfstaffel (Nacht), a training unit to initiate pilots into the mysteries of night ground attack. Operating from Staaken near Berlin we flew the FW190F-8, and this time our training was thorough.

At the bombing range at Jüterbog, south of Berlin, we carried out first day then night training attacks on targets marked for us by *Flieger Verbindungs Offiziere* (ground liaison officers). By the end of the course we were able to navigate ourselves at night to the target area at altitudes below 1,000ft (to avoid enemy night fighters). At a previously designated pull-up point we would start our climb to an attack altitude of around 8,000ft, at the same time warning the ground liaison officer that we

were coming. The aim was to be over the target at the correct altitude with our speed well down. We then called the ground liaison officer again and he would mark the target with flares. Once the flares were in view we would head towards them; as they disappeared under the leading edge of the wing close to the engine we would count 1 – 2 – 3 – 4 then roll the aircraft upside down. By putting one's head right back against the armour we could see the illuminated target and then we had to pull back on the stick until the target was in front of the Revi sight. During the dive, made at an angle of about 40 degrees, the propeller blades were set to fine pitch so that they acted as an airbrake to prevent the speed from building up too rapidly. As soon as the target was in the centre of the Revi we held it there for a few seconds, then we eased back slightly on the stick so that the bomb would clear the propeller and pressed the release button. For safety reasons the minimum release altitude was around 3,300ft and by the time we got there our speed was around 380mph; after the release we pulled out of the dive, then descended to below 1,000ft for the return flight.

During this type of attack it was easy to become disorientated, especially during the roll-over and pull-through before one was established in the dive. So considerable practice was necessary before we were proficient. Each new step was tried in daylight first, then at night. The carriage and release of a 1,100ft cement training bomb during such an attack marked the final phase of our night training.

At the beginning of February 1945 *Ergaen-*

Left: Faehnenjunker Feldwebel Franz Zueger, who flew night ground attack missions in Italy./*Zueger*

Below: A few FW190s were fitted with the FuG101 radio altimeter, which made it possible to fly safely at low altitude at night or in poor visibility. The downwards-looking aerials, one for transmission and one for reception, used the underside of the port wing as a reflector. *VFW-Fokker*

zungskampfstaffel (Nacht), like several other operational training units, was thrown into battle in a desperate attempt to stem the fast-moving Russian advance into East Prussia. Operating by day from Staaken and Rangsdorf near Berlin we carried out low level attacks on targets in the Zellin, Kalenszig and Klewitz areas. The Russian tanks were streaming across the frozen Oder River and we would attack them with 550lb bombs; the object was to score hits either on the tanks, or else near misses that would split the ice and cause the tanks to fall through. On other occasions we made strafing attacks and released containers of SD-2, and SD-4 cluster bombs. During these operations the Russian fighters gave us little trouble, but the light flak was murderous. During our four days in action every one of our aircraft was hit and we lost four pilots out of twelve.

In the middle of February I was sent to Italy, to join the newly-formed Third Staffel of Nachtschlachtgruppe 9; the other two *Staffeln* operated Junkers 87s, also in the night ground attack role. By the time I reached Italy the front was beginning to fall to pieces and we were moved around quite a lot. Typical of the airfields we used was that at Villa Franca, near Verona. By day our aircraft were dispersed in the surrounding fields, carefully camouflaged in small individual revetments made from piled stones. Looking after us we had a *Batterie* of light flak, with 37mm and quadruple-barrelled 20mm weapons. They were very good, and whenever enemy aircraft came near the field the gunners would give them a rough time.

The operational attacks we made against Allied positions in Italy differed somewhat from those we had made on the bombing range at Jüterbog. For one thing they were usually mounted against targets far beyond the front line so that there was no ground liaison officer to do the marking for us. In practice this meant that to achieve any sort of bombing accuracy we could attack only on clear moonlight nights. A further change was that instead of the half-roll and pull-through type of attack used during training, we used the simpler method of approaching to one side of the target and as it disappeared under the wing we banked into the dive; this enabled us to keep the unmarked target in view almost the whole time and the speed did not build up so rapidly when we entered the dive.

During the night operations the Focke Wulfs went out singly. Careful pre-flight planning was essential and there was a specialist navigation officer attached to the *Gruppe* to assist pilots. On our airfield we had a radio beacon which was a great help, both to provide an indication of drift on the way out and homings on the way back.

After releasing our bombs, we had orders to carry out strafing attacks on enemy road vehicles. Sometimes the lorry drivers would get a bit careless and drive with their lights on, which provided us with a bit of sport. But usually there was little to be seen at night over the other side of the lines. Nevertheless it was frowned upon if we came back with a full ammunition load so we would fire off a few bursts into the 'enemy' darkness, to keep everyone happy.

Typical of the night attacks we made from Villa Franca were those against Bologna, on the 22, 23 and 24 April to assist German paratroopers cut off in the city. These all followed a similar pattern. Since the target was only about seventy miles from the airfield, less than twenty minutes flying, we did not bother with a low altitude approach. Instead we climbed straight ahead and flew an almost direct route to the target at altitudes around 13,000ft, jinking from time to time in case there were night fighters about. The nights were clear and with a battle raging in the city we could see the burning buildings from some distance away. We were briefed to hit a group of buildings on the northern side, so that the paratroopers could get out. On each night we operated in full *Staffel* strength, making standard dive attacks with 1,000lb bombs; the buildings were flattened. On the way out and back we were fortunate to have assistance from *Freya* radar stations situated along the southern face of the Alps. As well as providing navigational help, these were invaluable in giving warning of the presence of enemy night fighters. Radio calls such as '*Kleine Eule von rechts*' (little owl – enemy night fighter – coming from the right) never went unheeded.

During the night operations we maintained strict radio discipline, using our sets only for essential calls. And whenever we did use the R/T, shortly afterwards on that frequency we would get the Allied propaganda people coming up: '*Kameraden der deutschen Luft-waffe, kommt zu uns . . .* ' (comrades of the German air force, come over to us . . .) Then would follow detailed instructions of how to reach certain designated airfields in order to surrender. Once that lot started we could not get a word in edgeways on the frequency so we had to change to a secondary. But within a minute of our making a call on the new frequency, up he would come again: '*Kameraden der deutschen Luftwaffe . . .* ' I must say, they were triers! But I never heard of any of our aircraft in Italy going over to the enemy.

Getting back to our airfield after a mission was always a bit of an adventure, because the Allied night fighters soon got to know where we were based and would lay in wait for us. So we had to use a little cunning. As each aircraft took off, the airfield lighting was switched off. Back overhead the airfield after a mission, we would flash our navigation lights to identify ourselves; my aircraft was number 8, so I had to flash my lights eight times. The people on the ground would acknowledge by flashing the runway lights on eight times. During the cross-wind leg, before turning in to land, we had to flash our navigation lights again, one long flash then two short ones; this too would be similarly acknowledged from the ground and gave us a final check of the position of the airfield. Then we would lower the flaps and undercarriage and, when established on the final approach for landing, flash the aircraft's lights long – short – long. On that signal the runway lights would come on and stay on until we were down. As soon as the aircraft had landed, however, the place was plunged into darkness once again. As we rolled to a stop at the end of the runway a motor cycle would pull round in front of the aircraft; following the dim red lamp on the rear, we would taxi back to our revetment. We lost very few aircraft to enemy night fighters; but several were wrecked in landing accidents, usually the result of a pilot making a bad approach and coming in too fast.

To make things as difficult as possible for the enemy night fighters trying to strafe our airfield, we altered our landing procedure frequently. The normal flare path used in the Luftwaffe comprised two green lamps marking the touch-down point, a line of six or seven white lamps down the right hand side of the runway, and two red lamps marking the end of the runway. Sometimes, by prior arrangement, the lamps were repositioned so that the reds in fact marked the touch-down instead of the stopping point; or the white lamps might mark the left hand side of the runway instead of the right. It all made things a little easier for us when enemy night fighters were about and sometimes they strafed in the wrong place.

During the final two weeks in April the German withdrawal from Italy became a rout. We made our final attack on 29 April from Thiene near Verona, then withdrew to Innsbruck in Austria just before the cease-fire was announced for German forces in the south, on 2 May. We destroyed our trusty Focke Wulfs, then disbanded our unit. Now there was nothing else to do but go home, so I began walking the 450 miles to Bremen where my wife was.

Below: An FW190A-8 seen carrying the experimental Blohm und Voss 246 *Hagelkorn* (hailstone) unpowered glider bomb, at Karlshagen in the summer of 1944. The testing of this weapon continued until the end of the war with various types of guidance, but it was never used operationally.
via Selinger

Right: Close up of the nacelle mounted 30mm MK103 high velocity cannon, fitted to the FW190F-8 for ground attack missions; the installation was not a success, however, and saw little operational use. *VFW-Fokker*

Below: During the summer of 1943 this A-5 was modified to carry a dummy LTF 5b torpedo. To enable it to lift this load all of the guns except the two wing root cannon were removed and a lengthened tail wheel was fitted. With the torpedo and two 66 gallon (300 litre) tanks, the FW190 had a take-off weight of over 11,400lbs (5210kg). Tests at the proving ground at Hexengrund near Gotenhafen were not successful and the torpedo-carrying fighters was not considered suitable for operations./*VFW-Fokker*

Left: An FW190A-5, experimentally modified to carry the 2,200lb SB1000 high explosive bomb; to provide sufficient ground clearance the lower fin of the bomb had to be removed. Yet even this was not the heaviest weapon to be carried by the FW190. In September 1944 specially modified FW190s of III./KG 51 carried out attacks on the bridge at Nijmegen following its seizure by American paratroops, using the huge SC1800 bomb which weighed just under 4,000lbs. The bridge was powerfully defended by fighters and guns, however, and escaped serious damage./*VFW-Fokker*

Finale

Left: This FW190D was unusual because it was one of the very few to carry underwing bomb racks./*via Girbig*

Right: The final version of the FW190 family to enter production was the Tank 152H, a major re-design with a lengthened wing for high altitude operations. Powered by a liquid-cooled Junkers Jumo 213 in-line, this fighter had a maximum speed of 472mph at 41,000ft, a performance which took it to the very limit of what was possible using a piston engine./*VFW-Fokker*

Below: Just before the end of the war the Tank 152H entered service and saw some action with Jagdgeschwader 301. This photograph shows aircraft of the unit's *Stab* and III. Gruppe lined up on the ground at Alteno bei Luckau south of Berlin and was taken in March or April 1945.

The following excerpts, taken from the flying logbook of Leutnant Helmut Wenk who flew Focke Wulf 190F-9 fighter-bombers with the Third Gruppe of Schlachtgeschwader 1, convey a vivid impression of the hectic series of actions fought to the north of Berlin during the final week of the war.

Date	Time, From To	Route	Enemy Activity (Fighters flak)	Results of Flight
27.4	1440 1540	Neubrandenburg – west of Prenzlau – Gollmitz – Neubrandenburg	Light flak, fighters	1 x 250kg container with SD-4 hollow-charge bombs released in the dive from 4,800ft, on the road through the wood near Gollmitz. Precise results not observed, but the bombs fell in the target area. Attacked a self-propelled gun from low altitude, results not observed. Air combat with four La 5s; the one fired at disappeared into a layer of cloud.
27.4	1850 1945	Neubrandenburg – west of Prenzlau – near Boizen – Neubrandenburg	Light and medium flak, fighters	1 x 250kg container and 4 x 50kg bombs released in the dive from 7,400ft, on the briefed target at the corner of the wood near Zervelin. Due to poor light, results not observed. Ten La 5s tried to intercept and fired at the second *Rotte*.
28.4	1635	Neubrandenburg – east of Neubrandenburg – Neubrandenburg	Light flak	Reconnaissance flight at between 3,000ft and ground level. Enemy armour and troops to the east and south-east of Neubrandenburg, seen to be advancing. Bad weather and rain showers, cloud base in places 700ft. After this report an operation was flown against this target, then the unit withdrew to Barth.

Below: An FW190D-9 taking off for a ground attack mission during the closing stages of the war, with an AB500 small bomb container under the fuselage. This aircraft is believed to have belonged to II./JG 26, which operated from Nordhorn at this time./*via Girbig*

Date	Time, From To	Route	Enemy Activity (Fighters flak)	Results of Flight
28.4	1805 1900	Neubrandenburg – east of town of Burgstargard – Barth	Light flak	1 x 500kg armour-piercing bomb from 1,300ft on the road through the wood on the outskirts of Burgstargard. Target hit.
29.4	1540 1625	Barth – Treptow – Barth	Light flak, fighters	1 x 500kg armour-piercing bomb on the road where columns passing, east of Treptow. Low altitude attack, hit observed. Air combat with Yak 3, no results observed.
29.4	1800 1850	Barth – Treptow – Barth	Light flak	1 x 250kg container and 4 x 50kg bombs released on the column at the previous target. Due to thick smoke, results not observed. Oblt Lehn (my wing man) crashed on take-off and killed.
30.4	1030 1140	Barth – Neubrandenburg – Barth	Nil	*Schwarm* leader became disorientated in cloud, ran short of fuel. 1 x 500kg bomb jettisoned.
30.4	1700 1745	Barth – east of Greifswald – Barth	Nil	The roads in the target area were found to be again in our hands and the roads in the enemy occupied area were all packed with refugees. 1 x 500kg bomb jettisoned.
30.4	1930 2015	Barth – east of Greifswald – Wismar	Light flak	1 x 500kg and 4 x 50kg bombs on a column of enemy vehicles heading for the outskirts of the town. Bombs laid accurately. Tanker vehicle hit, thick smoke seen clearly.
2.5	1400 1500	Wismar – Barth – Flensburg	Fighters, (Thunderbolts). Hit twice by own flak	Russians and English almost at airfield. Transfer to Flensburg.

Cease fire on 3.5.45 at 0800hours, on the orders of Grossadmiral Doenitz

FOLLOWING A PARADE WITH A SOLEMN ADDRESS BY THE COMMANDER AND THE SINGING OF THE NATIONAL ANTHEM SCHLACHTGESCHWADER 1 (WITH A TOTAL STRENGTH OF ONE *GRUPPE* OF ABOUT 30 AIRCRAFT), UNDEFEATED BY THE ENEMY, DISBANDED ITSELF INTO SMALL GROUPS TO MAKE THEIR WAY HOME, PLEDGED TO CONTINUE TO DO THEIR DUTY AND BUILD A NEW, BETTER, GERMANY.

FW190s serving in foreign air forces.

Left and right: After the war a few FW190A-8s, under the designation NC900, served in the French Armee de l'Air for a short time./*via Frappe*

Below: A pair of FW190s and a Spitfire of the Turkish Air Force, which received both types during the war./*IWM*

'Even the final decision of a war is not to be regarded as absolute. The conquered nation often sees it as only a passing evil, to be repaired in after times by political combinations.' *von Clausewitz*

Glossary

Luftwaffe Fighter And Ground Attack Unit Organisation

From the organisational point of view, the basic Luftwaffe unit for fighter or ground attack aircraft was the *Gruppe*, comprising three (later four) *Staffeln* each with nine (later sixteen) aircraft, plus a *Stab* unit with three or four aircraft for the use of the commander and his immediate personal staff.

A fighter (*Jagd-*) *Geschwader* comprised three (later four) *Gruppen*, plus a further *Stab* unit with three or four aircraft. The ground attack (*Schnellkampf-*, later *Schlacht-*) *Geschwader* was broadly similar, except that the fourth (*Ergaenzungs-*) *Gruppe* was an operational training unit for the conversion of pilots new to the role.

The *Gruppen* within a *Geschwader* were numbered in Roman numerals before the *Geschwader* designation; thus the Third *Gruppe* of *Jagdgeschwader 26* was abbreviated as *III./J.G.26*. The *Staffeln* within a *Geschwader* were numbered consecutively using Arabic numerals. Thus in a unit of the early war period comprising three *Gruppen* each with three *Staffeln*, the *1st*, *2nd* and *3rd Staffeln* comprised *I. Gruppe*, the *4th*, *5th* and *6th Staffeln* comprised *II. Gruppe* and the *7th*, *8th* and *9th Staffeln* comprised *III. Gruppe*. The *8th Staffel* of *Jagdgeschwader 2* was therefore abbreviated as *8./J.G.2* and the unit was part of *III./J.G.2*.

Regardless of his rank, the commander of a *Staffel* held the title of *Staffelkapitän*, a *Gruppe* that of *Gruppenkommandeur* and a *Geschwader* that of *Geschwaderkommodore*.

The basic *fighting* element in the Luftwaffe was the *Rotte*, or pair of aircraft; two *Rotten* made up a *Schwarm* of four aircraft; three *Schwärme* made up a *Staffel* of twelve aircraft. Ground attack aircraft were usually similarly sub-divided, though some units preferred the three-aircraft *Kette* as the basic fighting element.

Equivalent Ranks

Luftwaffe	Royal Air Force	USAAF
Commissioned		
Generalfeldmarschall	Marshal of the RAF	General (five star)
Generaloberst	Air Chief Marshal	General (four star)
General	Air Marshal	Lieutenant General
Generalleutnant	Air Vice-Marshal	Major General
Generalmajor	Air Commodore	Brigadier General
Oberst	Group Captain	Colonel
Oberstleutnant	Wing Commander	Lieutenant Colonel
Major	Squadron Leader	Major
Hauptmann	Flight Lieutenant	Captain
Oberleutnant	Flying Officer	First Lieutenant
Leutnant	Pilot Officer	Second Lieutenant
Non-Commissioned		
Oberfaehnrich	Officer Cadet	Officer Cadet
Feldwebel	Sergeant	Sergeant
Unteroffizier	Corporal	Corporal
Flieger	Aircraftman	Private